LIFE
AS A
RIVER

Memories & Reflections of a Die-Hard
Fly Fisher and Eco-Activist

MICHAEL MARX

Copyright © 2019 Michael Marx
All rights reserved.

LiveTrue Books, Imprint of Carroll Communications,
https://lauracarroll.com

The cover image from *Trout: An Illustrated History*, by James Prosek, appears by permission of Penguin Random House Books, Inc.

Excerpts and the snake card image from the *MEDICINE CARDS* by Jamie Sams and David Carson, published by St. Martin's Press are reprinted with permission of the Authors. Illustration by Angela Werneke. Copyright 1988 and 1999.

The image of Captain Willard from the film *Apocalypse Now* appears by permission of American Zoetrope Productions.

The photograph of Barnes Butte Lake is used by permission of Fay Ranches.

The photograph of a swimming fly fisher is used by permission of Ralph and Lisa Cutter (photographer). It appeared in an article by Ralph Cutter entitled "Wading Safely," on flyfisherman.com, January 24, 2014.

All images of artificial flies appearing at the end of each chapter in this book are products of Umpqua Feather Merchants and appear by the company's permission. Designers of the flies, when known, are listed at the conclusion of this book. The image of two grasshopper flies at the end of the Marriage River chapter was purchased from Shutterstock, 3/23/18, ID 49884922, standard license, photo by BW Folsom.

The Fly Fishing Glossary at the end of the book is used with the permission of Fly Fishers International. Some fly fishing terms were added and defined by Michael Marx where noted.

No part of this publication may be reproduced, stored in a retrieval system or transmitted in any form or by any means without the prior written permission of the author or publisher. For all eBook versions, including but not limited to Kindle, Nook, or pdf, this eBook may not be resold or given away to others.

ISBN 978-0-9863832-2-9
eISBN 978-0-9863832-3-6

Jacket design by Rob Williams

Dedicated to
Laura Carroll

Without you
    my skillful and dedicated editor
        this would have just been
           a collection of stories,
    verbose, in passive tense,
        lacking visual texture
            stored on my hard-drive
              until fate
            as it always does,
                crashed my computer
                    and all were lost forever
                      because it would be too hard
                to start over again.
    You are the person who
    encouraged me
        to learn to fly fish
            introduced me
                to the man
                who taught you
            then left me alone
        to immerse myself
            in my passion
        and trusted me
            to surround myself
                with the best of men
                  allowing me
                      to roam free
                      and always welcoming
                me back eager
                    to hear the stories
                which now are in this memoir.
              You are the river of love
                  that runs through me.

Contents

Foreword ... 7

Introduction and the Cast of Characters ... 9

Making Rivers ... 23

The Kid Goes Winter Fishing ... 29

Awakening to the Fly ... 35

It's Not Always about Catching ... 43

Never Take a River for Granted ... 47

Fishing the Deschutes Stonefly Hatch ... 53

Up the Rajang ... 61

The Roaring Fork River as Ally ... 77

Snake Medicine ... 83

"Mike Marx Is Dead" ... 91

The Odyssey: Utah, Wyoming, and Idaho in a Week ... 95

Raised by Whales ... 109

The River That Cannot Be Named ... 115

My Shamanic Journey ... 127

Fighting a Freight Train	133
The Fly Fisher's Dilemma	141
Mitch: The Tao of Rivers	149
The Marriage River	157
Tell Me a Fishing Story	163
Fishing for Lunkers	167
Apocalypse Now: A River into the Heart of Darkness	177
Fishing New Zealand	181
Unforgettable Moments in My Mental Creel	189
Alaska: Bucket List	199
Little Boy Fishing in the Greater Yellowstone	215
When the River Ends	225
An Old Fisher's Reverie	237
Acknowledgments	241
Answers to "Name That Fly"	243
What Does that Fly Fishing Term Mean? A Fly Fishing Glossary	245

Foreword

The first time I cast a fly rod I was on the Deschutes River with Michael Marx. As the sun dappled on the river, massive red-sided trout porpoised across the surface, their shoulders slicing the water like circling sharks. Not a bad beginning. Michael was teaching me to fly fish at one of his favorite spots on one of his favorite rivers. With the gentle gurgle and shushing of the river and the sight of those incredible fish, it felt like a scene from *A River Runs Through It*. Although nearly 20 years ago now, that day still feels very close—it felt nothing short of magical. That is, until I tried to cast. When I did, the movie screeched to a halt, and there I was, looking like an elephant trying to run an obstacle course. When Michael took a cast, he looked like a panther on the prowl.

Todd Paglia

I didn't even have my own rod at that time and I kept pushing our one rod back toward Michael. And cast after cast—first hitting a rock to the left of the trout, then driving the dry fly into the water at our feet—Michael gently insisted I take another shot.

"Ease off a bit and pause when you back cast," he whispered, never taking his eyes off the fish. Ten, maybe fifteen attempts later, I saw my fly doing something strange: flying. All of Michael's coaching had somehow gotten through. My fly floated through the air, then landing softly in perfect position. But where the fly landed now ran a very quiet stretch of river. Something about the last twenty abominable casts had scared every fish in this entire stretch of the Deschutes. I got in one good cast. Michael cheered. No trout was hooked, but I was.

I went on to learn to fly fish, at times becoming a bit of a fanatic, thanks to Michael. And it was only once I learned to really fly fish that I understood the generosity of that day. Those moments on the river when everything feels perfect are rare—and giving that moment away is a beautiful thing. That's Michael.

Who is *Life as A River* for? Fly fishers, for sure. From death defying spills, bucket list destinations, the frustration and reveries of life on the fly, this book has it all. For environmental and social change advocates, this book will inspire a meditation on change and how it happens, especially on the power of connecting across aisles, and even through fishing. Outside these circles, *Life as a River* is for anyone who wants to see our world change for the better. All who read it will see it's also about families—both the ones we are born into and our chosen families. And much more.

At the time of this writing, Michael and I have spent much more time in the office than on the river—but we are still working on that ratio. He hired me out of the law (thank you, Michael) and into the world of environmental campaigns, mentoring me in the office as well as on the river. The river of Michael's life runs deep—at play, at work, and in his relationships. All of these realms intersect and build like so many tributaries forming a single river. And it is a river that more than anything else, runs rich with generosity.

Todd Paglia
Executive Director, STAND
April, 2019

Introduction and the Cast of Characters

Like a river, my life began small. Each time a new tributary of experience entered the main stem, the river of my life changed and became bigger, more complex, more powerful, and at times out of control. The first time I learned to fish as a kid, I changed a little. When I became a Boy Scout and learned to backpack, camp, canoe, and teach nature merit badge, I changed a little more. When I became a competitive high school and college debater, and then started a summer camp for high school kids, I changed a lot.

When I went to Oregon for graduate school and joined a band of brothers, marijuana, rivers, whitewater rafting, and fishing changed me again. When I fell in love with the woman who would become my wife, my river became flooded with change. When she arranged for her friend and former boss to teach me to fly fish, my love for her and for this sport converged to transform me forever. Together they helped to set a course that would intersect with one last major tributary, environmental activism. That tributary entered at mid-life and completed the river that would define who I am and why I'm here.

I remember asking my osteoporosis-weakened and bed-ridden seventy-pound Grandma Holly (my first hero for starting one of the original nursing homes in eastern Washington) how she spends her hours day after day after day. "Honey," she replied, "I have my memories." She was unlucky to be permanently immobile, but lucky to have her mental lights burning brightly until the moment she died. Not so true for many elders I know. She taught me to stock up on memories.

Aging has a way of slowly erasing our memories, like old pictures continuously exposed to the sun. Memories lose their color and definition, merge with others, get jumbled up, and sometimes get totally erased. I wrote this book because I wanted to remember the moments that have helped shape me. I wanted to recognize and thank those who made those moments seminal for me. Writing it also creates a little insurance policy that in the event my memory goes completely south, I will at least have a book of stories and reflections that seem familiar and might occasionally spark moments of lucidity, assuming I remember how to read. Most of all, I wrote this book because of the fun it gave me to relive these adventures, big and small. Life reviews are supposed to put it all in perspective. This one just made me immensely grateful for my good fortune. At this point in one's life, gratitude should be the dominant emotion that inundates our souls, and for me it is.

I've written this book for myself, family and friends, but also for my fellow fly fishers and environmental warriors. Throughout the stories and reflections, I've tried to weave tips I've learned over the last thirty years about fooling, fighting, landing, and releasing fish. I've purposely promoted some well-known Western rivers that I think live up to their reputation and have intentionally been vague about others that my buddies would kill me for publicizing. For those new to fly fishing I've added a glossary of fly fishing terms at the back of the book to explain the meaning of words like tippet, drag, riffle, run, and stripping line. I've also taken the liberty of using fly fishing and rivers as metaphors and an excuse to expound on love and war. Lastly, I wrote each story to stand on its own so you could go where your currents of interest take you. Let me introduce you to who you'll read about in these stories and musings.

The Cast of Characters

One thing opens the doorway to my inner circle of friends—fly fishing. That circle contains a remarkable brotherhood of men. All successful, respected in their professions and driven to be among the best, we don't compete with each other, at least overtly. We love our wives and one-on-one we often wax eloquently about how lucky we feel to be married to such remarkable women. We love hanging out together, appreciate the humor and banter, and enjoy the pure pleasure of traveling and fishing together, if only for a week or weekend.

In a Leading Role

Jeff in Alaska, 2015

Jeff Wiles

Jeff and I met in graduate school at the University of Oregon when I worked as his assistant debate coach. Just a few years younger than me and though a student, he was the guy I really wanted to be—cool, one of the boys, smart, funny and someone who made others feel even cooler than they were. The "big fish hunter" among my cadre of buddies, in college Jeff bought a leaky dory and for two summers pursued a childhood dream to be a commercial salmon fisher. I think this had something to do with his love for his father and the times when they fished together for salmon off the Oregon coast. Years later, we would borrow his dad's boat and Jeff would thoroughly clean it up before returning it. As a roommate during his undergraduate years, Jeff was anything but tidy. But when it came to his dad's boat, he was anal compulsive as hell.

A born entrepreneur, after working in continuing education, Jeff started and grew a hugely successful business designed to train people to ace the postal exam. He then grew a business that provides licensing education in real estate, insurance, and mortgage lending. Now largely retired, he works as a philanthropist and private investor.

While he has a laser eye for detail in business, I love that Jeff says he can't tell a Hairs Ear from a Parachute Adams, yet he has a natural intuition for how to catch fish. Anything but a snob fly fisher, Jeff will use salmon roe to catch steelhead, herring to catch salmon, and god-knows-what to catch sturgeon. He has caught more species of fish than any of us.

I feel honored to have his friendship, and a bit humbled that I'm in his inner circle. He taught me that men can cry, feel scared, admit confusion, fuck up, and still be manly. He is one of two men in my life that I would cut a palm with a knife and merge his blood with mine as blood brothers.

Introduction and the Cast of Characters

Kirk on Grainery Lake near Grass Valley, Oregon, 2004

Kirk Hulett

Our wives went to junior high together and have remained close friends ever since. In the 1990s, four couples sat around our dining table at our forest home near Mount Hood talking about what makes relationships work. Kirk, the newest member of the group, seemed to give all the wrong answers to the psychologists and social workers at the table. He didn't appear to give a shit about what they thought, yet defended his perspective admirably. Kirk had a nonchalant flair for self-assured provocation in the presence of political correctness. I liked him immediately.

Kirk brutally broke into fly fishing on the Deschutes River. Impatience characterized his first encounter with the sport. At one point he slammed his reel in frustration on some rocks and bent it, which made him even angrier with himself. I thought he was never going to last in this sport. A year later, I went fishing with him and his dad on the Trinity River. At dusk, his dad sat in the car reading, and as I waded and casted my way toward shore in near darkness I looked upstream and saw him backlit by a pale night sky. Though still a novice, he casted like a pro and relentlessly pursued the last fish of the day. At that moment, I knew he was hooked.

As a securities lawyer, Kirk has sued major corporations for deceiving their shareholders. He has swum with the sharks his entire career. But if you want to see the true heart of this man, get him talking about his wife or kids. Once as we were driving back from fishing the Green River below the Flaming Gorge Dam, he pulled out a mixed tape he had created for his wife's birthday. The guy knows his music. The songs were smart yet laced with sentimentality for her. Like Jeff, I would cut a palm and clasp his as a blood brother.

Introduction and the Cast of Characters

Laura holding a Rainbow trout she caught and released on a private lake in eastern Washington, 2006

Laura Carroll

Laura and I met when I was working as a human resources consultant and she needed an internship as part of her graduate school program. We worked on a project involving the Myers-Briggs and became friends. She went on a couple of dates with two of my friends, and both asked me before they took her out whether it was alright with me. It seems my friends knew the future better than I did. We would see each other at group gatherings and occasionally meet for dinner as friends. After a couple of years of being just friends, one Sunday afternoon I happened to run into her walking by the house of another friend of mine. That day, we seemed to see each other in a "new" light. Before I knew it, we were heading to Calistoga for the weekend.

During our courtship we went on a fishing trip with her former boss and avid fly fisher, Danny Milligan, but have gone on few fishing trips together since then. A trip to Barnes Butte Lake was the last time we fished together. I blew it. She, another couple, and I had an agreement to leave at a particular time. When that time came, I was float-tubing at the other end of the lake and fish started rising around me taking midge emergers and duns. My subconscious rebellious teenager took over, and over an hour after our agreed upon departure time I kicked ashore to an understandably frigid reception. After that Laura and I agreed that I should just fish with my fellow "fishaholics." I still wish I had handled that day better. She is my best friend, and it would be fun to spend more days on a lake or river together with her.

Fortunately, like me, Laura loves her independence, and when I go fishing she seizes time alone to catch movies, see girlfriends or make trips she might not otherwise with me around. She loves that I'm hanging with my brothers and how I return from my fishing trips grounded and happy.

Introduction and the Cast of Characters

In a Supporting Role
(in alphabetical order by first name)

Christy Slovacek. A dear friend of Laura's and our neighbor when we lived on Mount Hood, Oregon, Christy and her husband built their home at the confluence of Clear Creek and the Sandy River. They have dedicated much of their lives to protecting the mountain from uncaring developers. Christy is a skilled outdoorswoman and an accomplished pianist, composer, and artist. During the nineties she studied with a modern-day Shaman and practiced shamanic journeying for several years.

Danny Milligan. Danny taught me to fly fish. He took me to Hat Creek and taught me the basics. Then he took me to Fall River, a spring-fed, crystal clear river, and took my education to the next level. When he retired, Danny bought eighty acres on the Williamson River outside of Klamath Falls where he caught the most incredibly beautiful and large Redside trout and hosted guests (like Laura and me) who wanted to do the same. Because of what he taught me and the joy I receive from this sport, I continue to feel an obligation to pay it forward with other novices.

Deb Streeter (an alias). Deb was my college girlfriend. Smart, athletic, quick to laugh, unafraid to cry in sentimental movies, generous and tolerant of my emotional immaturity, she was, and is, a remarkable person. She grew up with three brothers and thus was completely comfortable with the earthiness of two-week road trips living out of a camper, hiking into mountain lakes, floating and wading new rivers. If she felt queasy hunting night crawlers, impaling them on a hook, and cleaning the fish she caught, she hid it well.

Dick Recchia. The Executive Vice President and Chief Operating Officer of Mitsubishi Motor Sales when we first met, Dick and I started out as combatants in the largest international environmental campaign at the time. We found a common ground in our love of fly fishing and that connection proved invaluable to Rainforest Action Network's eventual victory in that campaign. A day on the Roaring Fork in Colorado helped us realize we could trust each other, find a mutually acceptable solution, and become friends.

Eric Chasanoff. I met Eric through his wife who sold me my first computer back in the early 1980s—a thirty-pound Compaq "portable." Whether it's building furniture, designing imaging software systems, competitive aerobatics in vintage planes, photography, fly fishing, long-distance open water swimming or making the perfect pizza, when something grabs his interest, Eric dives deeply into it. I turned Eric and his son onto fly fishing and he turned me onto float tubing.

Introduction and the Cast of Characters

Ernie Hulett. Kirk tells stories about the family taking a Sunday drive and pulling into an alley. His father Ernie gets out of the car, tells his wife, "I'll meet you at home," and then unlocks and drives away with somebody's car or pick-up. A repo man, Ernie also taught high school woodshop for most of his career. He had reached his seventies when Kirk gave him a fly rod for Christmas and he gave Kirk one—a mutual invitation to spend more time together. Ernie loved planning and shopping for fishing trips, walking the river bank, kicking around in a float tube, and one-on-one time with his son.

Jake Wiles. Jeff Wiles' son and my godson, Jake has the blood of a fisherman inherited from his father coursing through his veins. He grew up with either a fishing rod or a basketball in his hands and a passion for all things Nike. After playing as a star forward on his high school basketball team and graduating from the University of Oregon (Nike University), Jake became a social media marketing expert for Nike. As you will learn in this book, on a fishing trip with him Jake saved my life.

Louis Lexan. When I met him, Louis lived in a traditional Kayan Tribal Longhouse on the Rajang River north of Belaga, in Sarawak, Malaysia. The son of the former headman of the village, he likely governs the community now. He invited me to spend a few days with him when I was traveling up the Rajang River to learn about the extent and impact of Mitsubishi Corporation's rainforest logging operations. The trip changed my life and I owe Louis a great debt of gratitude for opening my eyes and my heart to the plight of threatened native communities.

Mitch Williams. Mitch truly knows his place on the planet and for decades has fought to defend it. We joined forces to try and stop Clackamas County from selling two hundred acres of a steep forested hillside near Mount Hood to fund a new golf course. Mitch introduced me to a couple of his favorite Sandy River fishing spots, and I returned the favor with some of mine on the Salmon River. He knows the ecosystem of Mount Hood better than anyone I know and learned by bushwhacking it, fishing it, and hunting for mushrooms. He even resettled beavers in their traditional river habitats on the mountain.

M'Lissa Trent and Hanalei Vierra (and Kekoa Trent Vierra). One of Laura's oldest and closest friends, M'Lissa instantly took to fly fishing. More than anyone I know, she could be a true Zen fisher, content to cast a hookless fly and fool but not hurt fish. For Hanalei, his Hawaiian roots make him a fisher by nature. Clinical psychologists by profession, they embrace opportunities to get out of the therapy setting and experience the freedom of being in nature. I introduced them to fly fishing on the White River in Oregon, hope to make many more trips together, and love them like a brother and sister (and Kekoa like a proud uncle).

Introduction and the Cast of Characters

Paul Franklin. If anyone in my circle of friends loves rivers more than me, it's Paul. He has dedicated more of his income, time, and emotions to protecting rivers, particularly the Deschutes River, than anyone I know. Paul loves people and they love him. He has an unparalleled ability to tell a story and end it with the perfect punch line or climax. Paul's tales feel like listening to a best-selling audio book comprised of intriguing short stories. Never for a moment do you think he is embellishing (even though he probably is) because Paul comes across as so authentic; his emotions are cast honestly on the table with abandon.

Phil McConville. Phil and I go back to my grad school days at the University of Oregon. He's part of my story by virtue of our history, hundreds of hours together on rivers and lakes, and his great sense of humor. One night after I ran him over hill and dale on the Deschutes near Warm Springs, Oregon, he said in his one-of-a-kind, low pitched, drawn-out-to-near-breathless expressions, "Oooooh, Gawd! I'm NEVER doing THAT again!" Dramatic. Self-deprecating. Funny as hell. After a week with us in Yellowstone and Wyoming, he declared, "I feel like I've been through a week of boot camp. I'm definitely a BOAT fisher." A damn good one too.

Wayne Lamprey. Wayne came into the circle through Kirk as a result of partnering on legal cases. Like Kirk, he relishes taking on corporate and government titans for their misbehavior. Despite his years of experience, when traveling with Kirk, Jeff, and me, Wayne plays the role of the rookie, light-heartedly asking questions, openly expressing wonder and eagerly photographing the different mountains, canyons, waterfalls, and wildlife we encounter. I like traveling with Wayne because he loves being in nature, rolls with the punches, knows good wine, appreciates good food, and has a great sense of humor and all the right values.

And last but definitely not least…

Artificial Flies. Without hooks, thread, feathers, foam, and fur, we would not be fly fishers. Which of us can enter a fly shop without dropping at least fifty dollars on the absolute must-have flies before heading to the river? Or never forget the exact fly that tricked that memorable trout? Artificial flies play an indispensable supporting role in this book. As a nod to their significance I've added an image of a fly at the end of each chapter. I've tried to make the selection relevant to the chapter in some way—sometimes obvious, sometimes not. See if you can guess the generic name of the flies before looking at the answers in "Name That Fly" at the end of the book.

*Nature Merit Badge for Boy Scouts
of America, circa 1964*

Making Rivers

When I was four years old, my parents bought the Grace Avenue house in a working class neighborhood in Spokane. It was tiny, maybe a total of 700 square feet. The house seemed to get smaller each time another sibling was added. Fortunately, the house came with a vacant lot. It was a weed infested wasteland, but I didn't see it that way as a kid. The neighborhood kids and I saw it as the wildlands that we ventured into through a broken down section of the old wire fence bordering our backyard. Our Narnia, the lot would transform into pretty much whatever our imaginations wanted it to be.

Sometimes we hauled plywood scraps and cardboard and built a fort, other times a clubhouse. Sometimes we loaded our Radio Flyer Sears knock off red wagons with rocks, marched to the edge of the lot, and launched a rock attack on the new kids across the street. Other times we chose sides among the neighbor kids and waged fierce cowboy and Indian battles. Occasionally on dark, warm summer nights we crouched among the weeds in a game of hide and seek.

More than anything, I made rivers in this vacant lot. I loved to watch moving water. I thought the way rain water ran down our side of the Nevada Street hill and flooded the intersection was the coolest thing. I would watch cars kicking up huge walls of water, mesmerized by the spray, the physics, the chaos and uncertainty of man-made vehicles crashing headlong into the uncontrolled force of nature, often flooding out their engines and rolling to a stop.

In the summer, after a late-day thunderstorm passed, it was time to make a river. I would carry all of my trucks and boats to the top of the vacant lot. The trucks became my digging and hauling operation. I didn't have toy engineers, so I would bring out my plastic green soldiers and conscript them into service. Though they were armed with bazookas, rifles and mine detectors, I didn't see them as warriors, just little molded men under my command creating a river system with channels, dams, and lakes.

I would drag our hose over to the neighbor's house, hook it up to the faucet nearest the north end of the vacant lot, and activate my mini Army Corps of Engineers with one purpose: to build a complex waterway of channels that all eventually led into my hand-dug reservoir. I wanted the river system to be as complex and long as possible so I could see the water flowing like a river. As the water softened the river and lake bottoms of my engineering work-in-progress, I would scoop out the mud and dredge the channel deeper. I'd stack up the mud on the imaginary river banks and let it harden into a smooth wall that deepened the channel even more.

Seeing muddy water in my river system with a skiff of foam on top bothered me initially. But since I assumed water was an endless commodity solely for my entertainment, and didn't realize that if

Making Rivers

it came from a neighbor's spigot they were paying for it, I just kept the river flowing until it cleared.

I could play in this world for hours. It was all mine. I made it run. I gave it a life and purpose beyond what anyone else but me could see. Sometimes I would let another kid play in my world, but I ran the show and he or she dared not mess with my creation. For the most part, though, I worked on my river alone, uninterrupted in my fantasy world.

I also remember making a river when I was a junior in high school and working for my third summer at Camp Cowles on Diamond Lake as a Boy Scout camp counselor. The youngest counselor on staff, I taught Nature Merit Badge. I loved to hang out at the Nature Lodge all day and help kids (many of whom were about my age) fulfill the requirements for that little patch. The badge required a restoration project, so I decided we were going to restore a river.

A bog covered in shallow grass lived at the end of the lake. When you walked on it, you could feel it give a little beneath your feet. A slow moving, six-foot-wide, two-foot-deep muddy little "river" meandered through the bog. I figured that if we could get the water moving faster, it would clear up and fish would come upstream. To me, rushing clear water and fish defined a healthy stream. This bog creek seemed like the perfect restoration project.

One morning my nature merit badgers joined forces with the soil and water merit badgers and off we went. Excited and into my idea, the badgers and I carried shovels, saws, six-foot thick wooden planks, hammers, nails, and an ax or two. We snaked in line for about a mile through the camp and down a road past some private cabins until we arrived at the end of the lake. Sunny, hot and clear weather made for a perfect day to restore a river. We worked up a sweat hauling big boulders and liked getting soaked as we positioned them just right in the stream. A couple of the senior counselors came along to help, and despite their age and superior knowledge of river physics, they treated the outing as my project. They gave advice and supervised the positioning of the boulders, but let me make the final calls.

We built a little wooden dam to generate some current. First we cut a large "V" out of what would be the top side of the plank and then fitted it into place with some big rocks holding it on the downstream side and a lot of little ones securing the upstream side. The water spilled through the "V" just enough to let fish swim upstream or down, or so we figured. The current it created was enough to generate a little turbulence, and the large free stone obstacles we positioned so perfectly pushed the water around like a gauntlet of warriors transforming an initiate into manhood. Suddenly, that little muddy stream had a personality. Before our eyes, it started to clear up and come alive. By the end of the morning we had resurrected a river. We even caught sight of a couple of little minnows that were probably there the whole time, but now we could see them.

A few weeks after we restored that little stream to life, I went down to see how our project was holding up and couldn't believe what I found. As I approached the scene, I saw that our dam had been thrown up on the bank. Some of the rocks had been moved around in a way that seemed intended to eliminate all currents. Rumors flew that a Camp Scoutmaster's delinquent kid and a couple of his friends had done the deed. With some effort, we put the dam back and moved the rocks into their previous positions, but I will never know if this "re-restoration" work survived since soon afterward the summer season came to an end and I headed back to school.

Making Rivers

I never found out who tore out the dam and re-muddied our river or why they did it, but I do know that today I wouldn't try to change that little murky flow of water. Now, I believe that not all rivers are meant to rush and fall and bang into and around boulders. Maybe the river we restored was just perfect the way it was—meandering slowly through a bog with just enough sediment to provide cover for the little fish that lurked below. Maybe someone who understood bog ecology better than us well-intentioned little Boy Scouts came upon our handiwork, cursed our ignorance, and spent an afternoon truly re-restoring the previously "restored" stream. One thing for sure, regardless of the wisdom of our restoration project, I'll never forget the feeling I had when twenty or so Boy Scouts and I surveyed our creation upon its completion and knew we had turned backwater into a river.

Looking back, that little project served as an early sign of things to come in my life. Twenty years later I decided to start volunteering for an environmental group. I first approached the organization, Friends of the River. They never returned my calls, so as fate would have it, I ended up at the Rainforest Action Network. Endless rain, evaporation, rivers and streams create rainforests. They house the most biologically diverse ecosystems in the world as well as thousands of tribal communities whose cultures date back tens of thousands of years. The more I learned about timber, cattle, and oil companies' assault on these forests, the more I felt an angry fire growing inside me. It really disturbed me to hear stories of how the erosion created by logging turned crystal blue rivers into muddy torrents flowing into dammed reservoirs that had displaced thousands of native peoples. I wanted nothing less than to stop the logging and tear out the dams so the rivers could flow freely again and the native communities could endure. I still feel that fire!

Winter on Clear Creek flowing past our cabin in the woods, Mount Hood, Oregon, circa 1998

The Kid Goes Winter Fishing

When I think back on Christmas mornings and opening presents from Santa Claus, one gift stands out. When I was about ten, I got a green metal, telegraphing, spin-casting rod. It ended up being the key that unlocked the door to a world where my dad wasn't yelling at me, I didn't have to think about homework, I no longer had to be the responsible big brother, and I could get as wet and dirty as I wanted.

I put that rod to use one time when my dad took me to Sheep Creek, a river north of Colville, Washington. He showed me the basics and then let me do my thing. Joe wasn't the kind of guy who was going to lord over his kid all day to make sure he was employing proper fishing techniques. It was just as well. His patience, or total lack of it, had a way of cutting an anxious edge into most of the things we did together when I was a kid. Like the time we were playing catch in the back yard and I dropped the ball once too often. The next thing I know he hurls the ball at me with full fury, missing my head by inches. Why my childhood ineptitude set him off makes for another story. Suffice it say, once he showed me the basics, it worked best to fish without him.

I remember getting caught in every damn branch on every damn tree that day, but still staying so fixated on catching a fish that it only made me more intent…and probably more entangled. Clearly I inherited my impatience from my dad. I probably caught a fish that outing, but I can't remember anything beyond my tangled line in the trees and how much fun I had fishing in a real river.

When I was fourteen, our family moved out of Spokane to a home we built on Hatch Road north of town. It sat on fifty acres overlooking a forested valley of pine trees. A ten-minute bike ride took me into Dartford Canyon to the coolest little stream called Dartford Creek. It ran through people's yards, ducked under the road through several culverts, then wound through some empty lots, woods, more yards, and finally emptied into Dragoon Creek, which emptied into the Little Spokane River, which emptied into the Big Spokane River, which emptied into the Columbia River. A little feeder vein, Dartford Creek had trout in it and for some reason not a lot of people fished for them. I felt like I owned that creek.

I can still see Dartford Creek in my mind. My younger brother Martin says he can easily recall its smell, especially the old wet logs we traversed to get to the other side where, of course, we thought the fishing would be better. He even says he remembers how the river would "breathe." It would pulse up and down like an aqueous chest expanding and contracting. I like the image, but I sure don't remember seeing anything like that. I do remember how the long grass used to hang down from the bank into the water on the edges of the stream. We knew that's where the fish would lie protected.

A favorite technique of mine involved casting a worm upstream and across the creek so that it floated just under the tips of the shoots of grass that dragged in the current on the opposite bank. Without fail, a little Rainbow trout would glide effortlessly from its shaded hold, grab the worm, realize it was hooked and streak downstream with a force far in excess of what you'd expect from a little ten-inch trout. Even on a steel rod it was a thrill. Of course steel lacks patience too and since my Zebco reel usually went bird's nest with a sudden jerk on the line, it was a good thing I was fishing with barbed hooks and catching little fish. As a meat fisher in my youth, it never even occurred to me that it was worth losing the fish just to experience the battle a bit longer, nor did I have that option with my gear.

I vividly remember a sunny winter day with about a foot of fresh snow on the ground. I was debating whether to go tobogganing on our hillside when I got sidetracked by the thought of spring. Of course that meant fishing. I daydreamed my way onto Dartford Creek, and began to think that fish must get awfully hungry in the winter months. What do they eat? The worms are living deep underground and we wouldn't see any grasshoppers for another six months. I decided to run an experiment. I was into experiments in those days. I won the eighth grade science contest trying to test whether white mice that lived and ate under a particular colored light for a month would prefer food that had that color when given a choice of the same food presented under different colored lights. The answer was no, and the reason is because mice are color blind, but I didn't think to even ask that question, and obviously the nuns didn't think of it either, so I won.

To run my winter fishing experiment, I loaded up my red and white fringed Naugahyde saddlebags with salmon eggs and cheese balls, and slung the bags over the rear fender of my Huffy bicycle like Roy Rodgers would saddle up Trigger. I mounted my metal steed and took off in a blaze of excitement, dodging the residual patches of ice on Hatch Road. I nearly crashed as I headed down into the shaded canyon. Finally having to walk my bike on the packed snow definitely made me a "fish out of water" on that winter's day.

I came to a culvert and parked my bike with the kickstand. All bundled up but with cold hands and red cheeks, I looked upstream to a pristine scene. The clear water almost looked invisible, and only an occasional surface current gave it away. The snow with not one footprint or blemish came right down to the water's edge on both banks. The sun magically glistened off the minute crystals coating the surface of the snow. I thought for a moment that I shouldn't disturb this perfect scene. Of course I did anyway.

A river in winter seems to relax. Snow seems to protect it from human intrusion. The fish are minimally active and a lot more efficient about how they expend energy to score a meal. The water runs pure, the algae die off, and the rocks and gravel "breathe" again. These days when I come upon winter scenes like this I just can't bring myself to exploit fish's hunger or disturb their winter's peace. I have no recollection of whether my experiment worked; only the peaceful beauty of that winter scene.

Thirty years later, Laura and I lived on Clear Creek near Mount Hood. In the winter millions of big wet flakes would start falling against the backdrop of two-hundred-foot Douglas firs and cover

The Kid Goes Winter Fishing

everything surrounding the stream. That scene transported me back to the time when I spent days fishing amidst the picture perfect winter's solitude of Dartford Creek. At times in the craziness of my environmental activist work, I have longed for the peacefulness and the simplicity of that winter's moment. The Dartford Creek scene remains glued in the photo album of my life.

*My parents' camper parked on Sheep Creek
where I first learned to fish years earlier, 1970*

Awakening to the Fly

To pay my way through college, I ran a summer debate institute for high school kids at Gonzaga University. In my high school days, only the upper middle class kids could afford to go to debate camps, and they ended up winning most of the debate tournaments including the state championships every year. In my senior year, my partner and I came close to winning the championship; we lost a split decision in the semi-finals to a team from the moneyed class. For financial reasons, we never considered the possibility of going to a summer debate camp. So in college, I decided to give high school kids of any social strata that chance.

Every summer I had about a hundred students for two two-week sessions. My spirited, Italian girlfriend Deb Streeter supervised the girls' dorm and my college debate partner, Greg Schultz, supervised the boys' dorm. We ran the sessions back to back. I made good money for a college kid. My staff of college debaters made a little money too. The kids learned how to debate at a reasonable price, and best of all, debaters who couldn't otherwise afford to go to a summer debate school became high school state debate champions. Many of them went on to become accomplished college debaters. Two called to thank me after they won the college National Debate Championship.

When the debate summer camp ended, I'd pay my staff, settle up with Gonzaga for room and board, and head out of town to go fishing for a month. My folks had an old 1941 blue International pick-up that my Grandpa Holland owned for years. When he died, my mother inherited it. My dad, being remarkably handy at everything mechanical, found an old camper that he restored and loaded onto the pick-up. That pick-up camper went all over the northwest and Canada for vacations, but mostly for square dancing trips where my folks would hook up with a flock of other couples for weekend square dance festivals. They would have tons of fun caravanning with their friends and do-si-doing to twangy country music and a tin can hollow-voiced square dance caller.

When the square dancing phase of my folks' marriage had ended, the camper still ran like a charm. So Deb and I would pack up our clothes and fishing gear, hit the local supermarket, and head off to camp together to sightsee and fish for a few weeks. Our first summer fishing trip taught me you could catch big fish on little rivers. The second summer fishing trip schooled me on the potential of catching them on tiny artificial flies and then letting them swim free again. After that I could never go back.

The Worm Was the Way

The first year Deb and I did this, we drove north from Spokane to Colville where we stayed the night to catch night crawlers in the moonlight on my uncle's well-watered lawn. In the darkness the worms came almost completely out of their holes and stretched out like thin little shiny brown snakes. We had to grab the end nearest their hole before they escaped with lightning speed.

After the Colville stop, we headed further north up to Newport and Sheep Creek, the same river my dad and I fished together as a kid. A quintessential trout stream, it flowed through a forested mountain valley with runs and riffles, and riparian guarding the banks. Its depth required a boat for some stretches (we had a little inflatable yellow raft with ridiculously tiny oars), but you could also hike the bank and find places to wade wet with tennis shoes.

I had a Fenwick fiberglass spin casting rod, and Deb owned the classic yellow Eagle Claw fiberglass casting rod. I confess I loved my spin casting days. I mastered hitting almost any spot I wanted across the river, even under a low hanging tree branch. In those days, it never occurred to me to use anything other than worms, salmon eggs, corn, and live grasshoppers.

Once on Sheep Creek, we tied on our hooks. We never pinched down the barbs, as they kept the worms on the hook—the bigger the worms, the better. Deb tied on her own hooks, and although she cringed slightly when she impaled a night crawler, she never needed assistance after her first lesson. Occasionally she would hold up her baited hook though and ask, "How's this look?"

We would usually catch our limits during the day. At night we'd dip a few of them in milk and egg batter, cover them with a flour and breadcrumb concoction, and throw them into a big frying pan with potatoes and onions. Complete with a little homemade tartar sauce and overly sweet Blue Nun wine, nothing tasted better on a warm summer's night after a long day of fishing. With my best friend and lover, the backdrop of clear indigo blue sky overhead, a thousand stars, a near full creamy moon, and a half million crickets for the soundtrack, the scene felt almost like a movie set.

One morning we got up early, made breakfast, headed down to the river, and saw a logjam we wanted to fish. Fishing a logjam means you have to drift into it from upriver to see well enough to reel in the line just before your worm gets pushed into the woody morass and lodged without hope of retrieval. That's exactly how we fished it, but after thirty minutes we gave up on that method. We decided to climb up on the logjam and try our luck. Deb had three brothers and grew up a tomboy. I liked that about her, especially in moments like these. I crawled up first and then turned to help Deb aboard. I hoped Deb would catch a nice trout on that logjam. She had earned it for being such a great companion to a fishaholic.

The sun had begun to hit the water, so we knew the shade of the logjam made this a good place to find fish. Deb cast slightly upstream and the lead weights took her worm right to the bottom. It drifted down slowly toward us and disappeared under the logjam. Since my uncle had told us that if we weren't losing gear we weren't down deep enough, we were prepared to lose the hook, line and sinker. Thinking it had floated far enough under us to entice whatever lurked down there, I said to Deb, "Reel it in and cast again."

She reeled in the line suddenly and then stopped. "It's caught," she said with a flash of frustration. Then BAM! Her whole rod bent tip down under the logjam. She barely had enough strength to keep from breaking the tip section as it hit against another log beneath us. She shrieked, looked at me and yelled, "What do I do?" She strained with her whole body to keep her rod from being ripped out of her hands.

"Hold on and let the rod fight him," I cried back with my heart pounding in my throat. I had never seen a fish in this river big enough to jerk the rod like that. She held on. The rod made several quick jerks to the left and then the right. I thought the fish might run, but it stayed under the jam. Thinking the fish might try to wrap itself around a branch to break her off, I shouted, "Try to reel it in slowly!" Even though she had thirty-pound test or more, one twist around a solid object would quickly shift the advantage to the prey.

As she struggled with all her strength to gain ground, I cried out, "Stand up slowly!" Shaking, she tried to stand. I clumsily got to my feet, put my hands around her waist to hold her, and told her to slowly lift the rod. The rod rose and then slammed back down to a vertically inverted position. "Hold on while I get the net!" I grabbed our woefully under-sized net and tried to position myself close to the water that was lapping up on a log about a foot below us. The water swirled with occasional windows of clarity to the bottom. I saw quick flashes of movement in and out of the shadows below. Deb held on, and her reel started to click slowly as she made a little progress against this uncontrollable force beneath her.

"I think it's getting tired," she said out of breath. Losing the fight now, the shadow below darted once, paused, and then darted again. Then it came out of the darkness into the swirling surface currents. A huge head came out of the water. As it broke the surface it rolled to its left and exposed the deep orange belly of a massive Brook trout. It was easily twenty inches, maybe more! Spots covered a flank that must have been eight inches deep.

The nose started to go down for one last dive. I lunged and reached with the net but just missed it. Seeing the net, it panicked and with a burst of new life dove straight down one last time. Then a huge rust brown tail splashed a wall of water at me as it broke the surface. I quickly wiped my eyes and prepared for the next rising. Body tensed, I crouched, this time ready to net this monster. I stared into the water expecting a second chance, but nothing. I looked at the rod and it was straight up in the air. Stunned in disbelief, "It broke the line," Deb uttered as she looked at the water where the fish had risen. "My drag was too tight and it broke the line."

"It was huge! Did you see it?" I exclaimed, also amazed at what we had just seen. She nodded her head, then shook it, as she looked back at the water, our fish long gone.

I only hope that incredibly beautiful fish lived. Research confirms that hooks dissolve after a few days. I want to believe it. In retrospect, I'm glad that fish escaped and left only a story. I would not want the memory of killing it, which we probably would have done. Instead, I like to think it would never be fooled again by a night crawler on hook and lived to an even riper old age under that logjam. But damn, that was a BIG fish!

A Huge Fish on a Piece of Fuzz

Yellowstone, 1971

The next summer after my debate school closed up shop, Deb and I loaded up the camper and headed to Montana to meet up with some of my college debate friends for a fishing trip to Yellowstone. I had barely graduated from being a worm and egg fisher to a spinner fisher when I read the Yellowstone regulations saying "barbless hooks, artificial lures, catch and release only." So I took out one of my favorite little silver spoons, pried off two of the treble hooks, pinched down the barb and started casting into a slow moving freestone river, the name of which eludes me.

Why I thought this mangled bit of shiny metal would fool anything remains a mystery to me. Obviously, I didn't truly appreciate the intelligence of native fish. I didn't even know a spinner was designed to imitate a minnow. To me it was just what you tied on the end of your line when you couldn't fish with worms or salmon eggs. I loved fishing, but had no idea of its possibilities.

After about an hour of unrewarded casts, an older guy called out to us in a Brooklyn accent, "Hey, you guys got a net?" I looked up at his nine-foot rod bent in a half circle with a brightly colored line I had never seen before diving at a steep angle into the river.

"Yeah, we do," I yelled back, holding up our cheap little net.

"I don't think that's going to be big enough, but let's give it a try," he said as he began to slowly reel in his line while walking downstream toward us.

Slowly a dark shadow emerged from the depths and took form just below the surface. It managed a few short runs as it neared the bank but gradually yielded to its fate. I handed over the net and with remarkable grace the guy quickly lifted the rod with his right arm, scooped the fish from behind with the left and brought this dark, wild, Cutthroat trout out of the water for us to see. The fish's body bent into a circle with its snout and tail both rising above the aluminum metal tubing. It left us breathless and in awe. That fish was HUGE!

My new hero bent down on his knees and lowered his trophy back into the water, holding the tail with one hand and handing me back the net with the other. He unclamped a pair of forceps from his vest and gently dislodged such a tiny hook I couldn't make out the lure. We watched in a reverential silence as he held the fish just below the surface, turned it on its side briefly for us to admire, held it…held it…held it…then relaxed his grip on the tail and watched it swim back into the shadows and disappear.

"What did you catch him on?" we all wanted to know.

"A black gnat on a size 22 hook with 6X tippet." He held out a tiny hook with a tiny black ball of thread attached to it.

"That's a gnat?" I asked in amazement. "You caught that huge fish on that little piece of fuzz?"

"Yeah, which is why I had to be so careful about landing him," he replied, fully aware that we were all but genuflecting in awe of his fishing prowess. Just then the clouds parted, shafts of sunlight shot through in a full array over the river, and as our prophet thanked us and walked back upstream, I experienced a moment of true enlightenment. You can catch huge fish on tiny imitation flies! I definitely wanted to know how to do that. In retrospect, like the young knight Parsifal, I saw the Holy Grail but failed to seize the opportunity it presented. It would take me another ten years to fully commit myself to learning to fly fish, but I had seen the Holy Grail: a big, wild Cutthroat caught on a barely visible black gnat!

Kirk and his father Ernie on Justesen's Lakes, 2004

It's Not Always about Catching

For several years my friend Kirk, his dad Ernie and I would head to northern California for three days of spring fishing. While we'd mostly go to Hat Creek, the Pitt River and Upper Sacramento River, the first time I went fishing with Kirk and Ernie we met on the Trinity River. As I watched Ernie climbing into his big green rubber waders with the rubber boots attached, I realized I should have given him a little advice before he went shopping for fly fishing gear. He bought the kind of waders you wear on commercial fishing boats—big, bulky rubber monstrosities. You don't fly fish in these waders, and you definitely don't walk on slippery rocks with smooth rubber soled boots attached to waders.

Sure enough, on that cold spring morning, the first time Ernie waded into a chilly river he quickly fell. I did not expect to introduce him to the sport like this. Worse, while drying out Ernie learned that in fly fishing you let the fish go and went into a state of total disbelief. Dumbfounded, he asked, "You mean we don't eat them? None of them? Not even one?" I bet he had visions of freshly caught, breaded trout sizzling in a big frying pan smothered with butter, onions, and potatoes that night. As an old-school fisher, he thought you don't put out all that energy and expense, achieve your objective and not enjoy the fruits of your labor. To fly fishers, why kill them when they will grow bigger and you'll have even more fun catching them again.

Old-school fishing brought most of the West Coast fisheries to ruin. Fishers caught gunny sacks of salmon and steelhead, took them home, ate some of them, and let the rest rot in the freezer or be thrown on the garden for fertilizer. For a while, thousands of fish seemed to magically come back every year, so people assumed the runs would endure no matter what. They believed fish would survive loggers destroying the tree cover that cooled and nourished their streams and the hillside erosion that would cover redds with silt. They'd be unaffected when skidders drove through their spawning beds, and they'd heroically make it through the spillways of dams to get to the sea. Somehow they would evade drift netting in the ocean, and gill netting three years later on their way home to where they were born, which of course would be ruined by more logging or development. Throw in water diversions to feed California's burgeoning population and compensate farmers for its increasingly common droughts, and the result? Extinct wild, native steelhead and salmon runs. So much for nature's magic act.

Ernie started fishing too late and fished too rarely to really get the knack for fly fishing. A good sport, he loved to fish, and especially loved this experience with his only son after years of not spending much play time with him. The Christmas before the first trip we made to the Trinity, Kirk and Ernie coincidentally surprised

It's Not Always about Catching

each other with fly rods and reels. This gift exchange subconsciously said to each, "Time is short. Let's get about being friends."

I didn't totally realize the emotional current that ran below the surface of this adventure until later. My impatience with Ernie subsided when Kirk reminded me that his dad's a "big boy," over six feet tall, two hundred pounds, seventy-five years old, out of shape with two knee replacements. It took me awhile to cut loose from wanting him to catch fish. When he didn't follow the tips I gave him, it totally frustrated me. Even when a tip did produce a fish, he rarely seemed to employ the tip again. I began to think he felt nervous about actually having to land, de-hook, and revive the fish without killing it.

It finally dawned on me that it wasn't up to me to make sure Ernie caught fish or had a memorable trip. In fact, the more I tried to make that happen for him, I realized the more it undercut the experience he wanted. Maybe at seventy-five I won't need to catch fish either (although I doubt it). I've speculated that as one moves up the ladder of fishing enlightenment, you pass from bait fisher (kill 'em), to lure fisher (kill 'em), to barbless hook fly fisher (traumatize them), to no hook fly fisher (fool them). I've thought about clipping off the point of the hook at the shank and fishing for a day with the idea that all I'd experience is the sight of the take, the sudden jerk of the line, the quick release and the mild mental euphoria of knowing I fooled a fish and left it unharmed.

I haven't been able to do this, and I wonder why. Maybe I don't know how many fish I'm going to catch so I have to make sure I don't waste an opportunity. More than a "take junkies," maybe I crave the excitement of fighting them, or said more romantically, dancing with them as they leap and charge, run and dive. Maybe I need to have the complete experience of selecting the right flies, casting the line to rising fish, setting the hook just as they take it, getting them on the reel and eventually in the net, taking the hook out and seeing how big and beautiful they look when reviving them and letting them swim away. Maybe I just haven't caught enough fish yet.

Can my ancestral cellular programming be satisfied with just the experience of the take? I don't know. However, when I read an article that suggests fish do feel the pain of the hook and stress when fighting for their lives, and about one in ten dies after being released, it throws a big messy black spot of yang in my clean white field of yin…and I don't feel like such a purist. Sometimes I fantasize about gearing up with some cool guys and wonder what I'd say when they tell me that they clip off the hooks. Could I truly become a Zen fisher? Hmm.

*Photo by Lisa Cutter from Ralph Cutter,
"Wading Safely," flyfisherman.com, January 14, 2014*

Never Take a River for Granted

The second time Kirk, his dad Ernie, and I fished together we met in Burney, California where I first learned to fly fish on Hat Creek. I had always fished below the power station where you get lots of nymphing action and often incredible dry fly action with light tippet and tiny imitation trico spinners. Unfortunately, over the years too many novice fly fishers like me waded this section to get their first lesson, causing the trout to move further down where it makes a wide, deep, meandering bend. The water slows down, and you can spot the working fish from the bank. They can usually spot you too, unless you go totally *Curtis Creek Manifesto*—on your belly. That book has introduced many of us to fly fishing and preaches the value of stealth.

In the stretch of river below the power station, I remember a typical scene of about ten to fifteen guys in one hundred yards of water. Too many urbanites too comfortable with crowding eventually killed the wildness of this stretch of the river. Instead of fishing there, we decided to fish above the power station. Green Drakes were coming off the water, which boded well for fishing both emergers and dries.

Ernie took the section closest to the car. Kirk took the next stretch where we saw some surface action. I walked up to where I saw a wide riffle. I love riffles. In this section dries weren't coming off yet, so I did what Danny Milligan had taught me on the lower section a few years earlier. I decided to high stick nymph fish. Psyched, I tied on a fly. Just thinking about nymphing the entire riffle all the way across the river made my hands shake with anticipation. I stepped to the edge of the river and began to make small casts upstream, followed by a slight mend so the fly dead drifted. Nothing. I took a small step into the river, cast out another three feet or so and began to work the riffle.

Ten minutes passed, and I found myself close to mid-stream. Still only knee deep with the water rushing by me with some force, I expected to hit a trout any second. As I totally focused on the indicator, all of a sudden I got a hard, quick jerk at the end of the drift. With my heart pounding so hard and fast I could feel it in my temples, I quickly got the fly back upstream and repeated the same drift. I made cast after cast after cast, stupidly thinking that fish could be fooled after being pricked with a hook.

The fever of the hunt overtook the futility of going after the known, and I decided to continue across the river. With my heart still pounding, I decided to take another step and cast into new water. So intent on getting the fly back in the water, I didn't think to look down.

Woooosh! I went under water, and the current pushed me from behind through a deep hidden chute in the riffle. I saw the surface about six feet above me. What happened to my perfect riffle in knee-deep water? How could I not see a twelve-foot chasm in the riffle? Deep in the river and a foot off the bottom, I half kicked and half walked in my boots and waders. I held tightly to my five-hundred-dollar rod with its two-hundred-dollar reel and fifty-dollar fly line.

My life didn't flash before my eyes, but I definitely remember asking myself a flurry of rapid fire questions: "Can I swim in Neoprene waders and big felt-soled boots? Should I release the suspenders to keep the water in my waders from pulling me down? Did I remember to wear a belt or to tighten it sufficiently around my waist? Did I ever do a waders swim test?" Then this command grabbed and shook me: "Get your ass to the surface as fast as you can!" I quit water-walking on the bottom and started kicking feverishly. Fully submerged with one hand committed to my rod, I did a one-handed breast stroke and made headway toward the surface.

Fortunately, I was in Hat Creek, not the Deschutes River, and it turns out that Neoprenes are predisposed to float. I stayed relatively calm and swam with the current until I hit the surface. It took another one hundred feet or more of some serious leg and arm motoring to get to the steep, eroded bank. After several failed attempts, I grabbed a bush that didn't dislodge with my weight. I hugged the bank like a long lost friend.

When I finally climbed up and stood on the bank, the sun and air seemed to say "Welcome back to land, you idiot!" I took off my suspenders, emptied out a gallon of water from the upper section of my waders, and shed my wet shirt, vest and hat. I tried to stop shaking. I could just imagine Kirk watching his buddy floating by with a fly rod in his hand on his way to the Hat Creek dam.

I looked back up the river to see how far I had drifted. Not as far as it felt like I had, but far enough for this lifetime. I looked downriver to see what I had escaped. It actually looked relatively harmless, assuming I was wading above water and breathing. Then I saw something in the water. Even with my eyes still a bit blurred, I could tell it looked like a fly box. My fly box! "Oh, great," I moaned. Since I'm one of those guys who buys too few fly boxes and loads them with too many flies, that little clear plastic container had at least $250 worth of flies in it.

I took off running down stream, still holding my fly rod. I yelled to Kirk to help look for a long branch so I could fish out my fly box. We madly scrambled around for a branch long enough, found an old limb and began to try and coax the fly box to shore. You probably know the routine. First you try to lift the box with the limb, but it keeps falling off. Then you try to brush it to shore, but it keeps sinking temporarily. Then you realize you need to create a little current of your own. So you start sweeping the water in front of the fly box like they do in the sport of curling. A lot of diligence, a little patience, and finally you get those fly purchases within reach. This too is fly fishing.

I've looked up at the surface of a river more than once. Another time I was floating down the Deschutes in a little inflatable Tahiti. Wanting a little solitude, I lagged behind my flotilla of friends in rafts and drift boats. Not smart. In a pot-induced altered state, I felt in tune with the river and leaned back against my life jacket, which was folded behind me, feeling the sun on my sun block-covered white skin. Also not smart. I was going through a small rapid when suddenly it didn't feel so small and the Tahiti lurched precariously sideways into a decent-sized standing wave. It flipped, and under water I went. I looked up and saw my inflatable kayak about twenty feet ahead of me, floating fast downriver.

Like before, my life did not flash before my eyes, but this time I realized this *was* the Deschutes and I *didn't* have a life jacket (or buoyant neoprene waders) on. I heard a familiar voice from an inner drill sergeant (or was it my dad?) yelling, "Get your ass to the surface as fast as you can!" No rod, no waders, and no boots could slow me down this time. With just gym shorts and an adrenalin rush of fear, I did the same breast stroke that saved me on Hat Creek, only this time I swam with the power of a person who wants to live and knows this is not a given at this moment. I hit the wavy surface, took a huge breath, and went Johnny Weissmuller (as in the original Tarzan when he outswam a jungle crocodile to save Jane).

With the current on my side, I got to the life jacket first and wrestled it on. Whew! Within a couple of minutes, I located the paddle, grabbed it and went for the Tahiti. In a moment of stoner's luck, the Tahiti stalled in a large, but manageable eddy. It came back upstream near shore as I moved downstream, and thanks to a desperate strong side stroke, the Tahiti and I had a joyous reunion.

I bet anyone who has fished or floated big rivers more than once has uttered the line, "Never take a river for granted." Those Class II or III rapids can make you pay if you let your attention stray. Rivers have a way of purging the disrespectful from the gene pool. They teach us vigilance. Having used a couple of my nine lives getting to shore or back in the boat in one piece, I like to think I've learned my lesson.

One of the many wild native Redside trout I've caught during the stonefly hatch on the Deschutes, circa 2010

Fishing the Deschutes Stonefly Hatch

In the morning on a warm mid-May day, thousands of the biggest nymphs in the Deschutes River start crawling underwater toward shore. They emerge from the subsurface to find a rock and dry out for few seconds. Then the outer blackish brown exoskeleton bodysuit they wear all year long cracks down the spine and a two-inch stonefly emerges. It bears little resemblance to what crawled out of the watery depths.

Two different flies constitute the famous stonefly hatch on the Deschutes. Orange and about three inches long, the salmonfly requires two sets of wings to carry itself across the river when it looks for mating action. Smaller and brownish yellow, the golden stonefly has two wings, one on top of the other on the fly's back. Golden stoneflies love to hang on reeds and bushes near the shore, but like their cousins, they can't help making a trip across the river to check out the mating action. This trip often gets these flies into trouble since a gust of wind in the wrong direction or a miscalculation in its flight plan could mean a potentially fatal water landing.

If they make it to the other side, they get down to business. You'll often find one fly perched on the other fly's back engaged in the insect version of a one-night stand, doggy style. Stoneflies don't have much time to enjoy the sun, find a mate, get it on, become pregnant, oviposit some eggs in the river, and flounder on the surface in exhaustion for a few seconds before a huge trout blasts through the undercurrents and scarfs them down in a single gulp.

During the stonefly hatch on the Deschutes, each day a new wave of stonefly nymphs finds the beach, escapes their exoskeletons, and takes to the air about a thousand yards farther upstream than the day before. They finally reach Warm Springs, the Indian reservation, away from the crush of fishers that coalesce around Maupin. My buddy Paul Franklin had told me about a stretch of water at a turn-out where you can park, check out the river, examine the bushes for flies, get your waders on, rig up, and work the next half mile of steep terrain along the bank upriver. One mid-week day in late May, I drove there singing back-up vocals to Springsteen's *Born to Run* blaring in my silver Toyota pick-up. I parked where instructed, walked over to the river and saw the warm sun reflected off the surface. I didn't see any other fly fishers around, so I went to the bushes near the water's edge. Sure enough, I spotted about a dozen salmonflies and golden stoneflies hanging on to stalks of the long thin weeds. I know you're not supposed to do this, but I picked one up, flicked its head with my finger nail to stun it, and threw it into a feeding lane about eight feet off shore. It floated past one bush, kept on floating, floating, flailing to get itself off the water and back to shore when suddenly I saw and heard a loud splash. The fly disappeared. My heart started pounding. I had never seen a take like that. Wow—so aggressive!

Envisioning the huge fish that must have taken that fly, I hurried back to my truck and changed into my waders. I rigged up my line and put on 4X tippet, which normally I would only use for nymphing, but anything lighter was sure to snap with a take like that one. I clipped upriver. After about fifty yards I saw a little path down to the water. Of course the path meant everyone stops there, throws out a line, and if any fish remain they've encountered every artificial lure imaginable and won't be fooled by me. Even so, I couldn't get my line out fast enough. I made a cast upstream. Nothing. Again. Then again. Nothing. I fed line out under the bushes downstream. Nothing. Surprised but undaunted, I moved on. This went on for about twenty minutes.

After years of playing out this same scenario, I know now that in situations like this I get completely focused and impatient. I expect action under every bush. I've already caught a dozen fish in my mind before I've seen any real action. My impatience generally causes me to get a little careless. So focused on getting to the prize, I forget that I have to slow down, sneak up on the fish, think about my cast, check the fly on the water to make sure it floats properly, and make the first cast count. I find it hard to sit under a tree and watch a stretch of river to see if anything is happening when I have the "big splash" tape playing over and over in my head. I feel native impulses from 100,000 years ago triggered in me, and the primitive hunter memory wants that fish, as if I'll starve tonight if I don't land it. I remember the same thing happening when I shot my first (and last) deer. "I became a Neanderthal again."

I decided to hike back up the hillside. I leaped over an eroded chasm, found a little deer path and followed it upriver. I stopped high on the plateau and looked out across the valley. I looked up and saw charcoal-colored rim rock rising up a thousand feet. Pyrotechnic granite pillars stood one after another with a lone hawk catching the updraft while hunting for mice. I forgot fishing for a moment and tried to burn the panoramic image of this scene into my brain. As an ex-Catholic, sometimes I think that unless I truly appreciate the miracle I am witnessing and am now a part of, the fish gods won't find me worthy to touch a trout. So I try to remember to look around, take in this miracle of billions of years of evolution, and say "thank you" from the innermost reaches of my soul. For my pagan ritual of gratitude and awe, I dip my fingers in the holy river water and touch my forehead, my eyes, and my lips. I pause for a moment and then start pulling off line for my first cast.

I followed the path back down to the river. A long slow section proved unproductive so I decided to move upstream again. Traveling the river bank felt more treacherous; I climbed over fallen trees, under dead branches, and through tunnels in the tall bushes. As I was untangling my rod from grabby vines, the words of guide Troy Bachmann of Welches, Oregon, came to mind: "If you don't have spider webs in your teeth, you're not fishing where the big ones are." Bushes, brambles, vines and thorns befriend the tenacious, filter out most fishers, and protect the fish.

As I was tripping my way through nature's obstacle course, I heard occasional splashes beyond the bushes. I came into a small clearing and just knew this thirty feet of river would bring some action. Forcing myself to sit on the edge of the bushes, I tried to stay low and out of sight. Upstream a little ways, I saw a floundering golden stonefly trying feverishly to get itself off the water. BANG! The take created a huge water explosion. So sudden, so vicious—that fly was gone.

It took a few seconds to get my heart rate back close to normal. I quickly pulled out a new stonefly, clipped off the previous one and made the exchange. I carefully greased it with floatant, crouched, and began to walk on my knees toward the water's edge. Then I pulled off enough line to land this fly in the same exact feeding lane the natural one had traveled. Keeping my rod tip down to not give any possible cue to my quarry, I crept closely enough to position myself for a cast upstream. I knew I would get one shot at this, so I mentally rehearsed the cast. I lifted the rod tip and held the fly in my hand. Then I launched the fly with a roll cast. It wasn't perfect, but I landed the imitation in the lane with a splash. While normally not the preferred landing for most flies, stoneflies don't land gracefully.

I pulled the slack out of the line and stared at the imitation floating toward the same point where the fish took the fly. I flicked the fly to simulate a little desperation. As it approached the target zone, I held my breath, ready for the take. Nothing. I couldn't believe it. The fly floated into and out of the contact zone. I wondered if I would have another chance to cast to this fish. Could it possibly be full?

The fly continued to drift just a couple of feet out from the first large branch that hit the water about ten feet out from shore downstream. I gave a quick mend thinking I might have six more feet of drift before having to retrieve the line. The mend accidentally twitched the fly and BAM—the fly was gone! My floating light green line was screaming off the reel and curving out into a fast current in the middle of the river. I let the line run off the reel, praying that I had set the drag properly. Then twenty feet farther upstream from where my pale green floating line disappeared below the surface a twenty-plus-inch wild Deschutes Redside trout rocketed three feet out of the water with my line attached.

The fish splashed down and then raced full speed downriver with the current at its back. I knew one false move and the line would snap. A 4X tippet suddenly seemed awfully naïve on my part. I stood up and tried to glide carefully out into the water. If I had any chance of landing this fish, I had to wade and get out beyond the line of branches. I used a technique Paul Franklin taught me; tilt the rod tip toward the bank with the hope that the pressure would eventually lead the fish to follow. It seemed to work because the fly line started running off the reel at a slower pace. My left hand was poised to take the reel, but I dared not touch it. I had lost Deschutes Redsides before by unintentionally getting my thumb too close to the reel handle as it rapidly unwound. One collision between thumb and reel, no matter how small, would snap the tippet.

The trout slowed just enough that I reeled a couple of turns, thinking it hovered nearer the shore. Then the line went slack for a second and I realized this fish was charging back upstream in the slow water. I stripped the line in like a madman. I cursed my left arm for not being more coordinated, but I was not going to lose this fish. My line was falling in chaos on the water but I still had tension. Then a jerk and the fish took a hairpin right turn and headed back for center stream. Another leap totally out of the water, and then a dive and run back downstream ensued. With the wet line racing through my fingers, I tried to create just enough tension so that when it hit the reel it would be a smooth transition to the friction of my drag.

The line hit the reel. The fish ran for a second and then slowed. I reeled. It jerked downstream again and stopped. I reeled a couple of turns. Paused. I reeled a couple more turns. Another pause. Another couple of turns. I felt every muscle in my body saying, "This fish is not getting off." It moved. I countered. I felt the opening for a series of rapid retrieves. Then a quick run. More rapid retrieves. I held the tip of the rod high and steady, not assuming this fish was already landed. I had lost too many fish on the Deschutes coming up the shoreline and suddenly breaking for one last escape run. I wanted to see this fish and know that for once when it mattered most I had done everything right. The branches concerned me;

I didn't know how deeply they dipped into the river, and I didn't want this fish to get tangled in a pine bow and escape. Just when I started to suspect the fish was indeed tangled, it exploded for one more run toward center stream and freed the line.

I swear this went on for more than ten minutes. Maybe not, but it took all the discipline I could manage to stay physically attuned to every little movement in my fly line. At one point when the dry line was almost totally back within the limits of the guides of my rod, I knew this fish was very close. I reminded myself that a wild fish, exhausted from the battle, always has one last run just as its captor comes in sight. Sure enough, the end of the dry line was within two feet of the last guide and the fish bolted right at the last limb. I quickly directed the tip of the rod to center stream and downward, hoping to keep the line from tangling on the last branch in the water. The fish dodged out and then back. I retreated a step and almost fell, but managed to turn the tip smoothly toward shore and down again to avoid the half submerged limb.

That was the last run. I slowly reeled it in. Without a net, even an exhausted wild trout is tough to get into your grasp. After a couple of failed grabs, I feared I would have to bring the fish to the shallow water to get control, but then I grabbed it with my thumb and forefinger around the shoulder. I couldn't get my hand around it, but it was tired enough to let me roll my hand under it while the other hand laid down the rod and quickly removed the imitation stonefly. While one hand supported the lower half of the fish, the other encircled it just above the tail. I held it in the slower current and could see the fright in its eyes. The gills were breathing quickly. Escaping bubbles told me that foreign air was being expelled and this wild miracle was again breathing only water. I dislodged the fly.

I held that fish for several minutes, watching its gills breathing in oxygen from the water and slowly returning to their normal rate. It had a beautiful red stripe and dark brown belly. With the tip of my finger at its nose and my forearm beside its body, I measured seventeen inches to my elbow plus another four beyond that. Such a strong fighter, yet in my grasp it seemed so vulnerable. I felt an incredible obligation to be patient and make sure I didn't release it too soon. Wild trout will sense an opening and escape your grasp, only to turn belly up further downriver from exhaustion. That was not going to happen to this fish. It was too beautiful and fought too bravely to lose its life in battle. As I held it, I gave thanks for the incredible encounter we just had. I had been given a gift to hold this wild, probably never caught, five-year-old product of 10,000 years of evolution.

That fish and I went into a joint state of meditation. I knew it was going to live. Calm and resigned, it sensed it was going to live. With my right hand I slowly loosened my grasp and then did the same under its belly with my left. It shot out of my grasp with a couple of quick aqua-dynamic power moves and headed back to its place in the river.

I stood up, but then a little dizzy, fell to my knees right there in the river. I looked up and raised my arms to the sky, overwhelmed with awe and gratitude. As if completing a ritual, I dipped my hands into the Deschutes, washed off my sweaty face with its coolness, and took a long, deep breath.

I've caught other wild Redsides with stoneflies, but I'll never forget the one that made me feel like I was connecting with the mystery of evolution in the deepest possible way. The experience of seeing, touching and releasing such a remarkable piece of living art will always blow me away.

Louis Lexan and a moss deer that he shot during our hunting trip into Sarawak's rainforest, 1991

Up the Rajang

Before leaving for the 1991 World Rainforest Movement (WRM) meetings in Bangkok, Thailand, I wrote in my journal that this didn't feel like an ordinary trip. It felt significant to have the chance to meet leaders in the WRM, facilitate meetings between them, and see whether I wanted to play more of a role in this movement. I had also scheduled an extra week to fly to Malaysia and get into a tropical rainforest. At the time, I had no idea that where I would end up would change my life forever.

I would be attending the meetings with Randy Hayes, the infamous Executive Director of the Rainforest Action Network (RAN). A brilliant coyote, it took him two months to respond to my letter a year earlier offering to provide free consulting to RAN.

When he did, he didn't care that I had no environmental training or knowledge of rainforests. I remember him saying to me, "I know rainforests. You know business management. It's a good partnership." I offered to donate a day a week. Then after a few months, I was donating two days a week to this young band of eco-warriors. A year later, I sat on RAN's Board of Directors.

On the plane to Bangkok, Randy informed me that in their last meeting the groups that comprised the WRM agreed to launch an international boycott of Mitsubishi Corporation. Mitsubishi was logging the homeland of the Penan, the last hunter gather tribe in Asia. He planted the idea that RAN should take over the leadership role of the International Boycott Mitsubishi Campaign. The campaign sat on RAN's back burner with a few modestly organized and attended local demonstrations. He thought someone with business and marketing savvy could turn it into RAN's first big international campaign and establish RAN as a key player in the movement. In his mind, I was just that person. I didn't know what I thought, but it seemed like a stretch.

I facilitated sessions between representatives of the World Bank and WRM, and picked up the issues quickly. Within a couple of days, a German radio station was interviewing me about why we considered the World Bank to be the most environmentally destructive institution on the planet. I knew enough to explain how the World Bank was facilitating the transfer of resource wealth of the undeveloped south to the elite classes of the industrialized north. The bank gave countries loans to build dams (that destroyed rivers and displaced tens of thousands of native people) to generate electricity for factories that could produce cheap products for sale in the industrialized nations. But dams in rainforests silt up quickly, becoming useless and leaving the country with huge debts to the industrialized lenders. The only way to pay off the debts was

Up the Rajang

to liquidate their natural resources (like rainforests) as fast as possible, which of course flooded the market with an overabundance of timber. This kept prices low for the north and revenues low for the south, which perpetuated the giveaway to the industrialized lenders. The World Bank was orchestrating a brilliant macro-economic Machiavellian strategy that sold developing countries first-world aspirations yet perpetuated their third-world status.

While at the Bangkok meetings I asked Yoke Ling, a leader of WRM and a famous female activist from Friends of the Earth (FOE) Malaysia, where I should go to see the rainforest destruction in her country. I knew Mitsubishi had operations there and it had sparked conflicts with native communities. The nonprofit organization Earth First! had just orchestrated a very highly visible and illegal direct action at a major log loading port in East Malaysia. They locked themselves to loading cranes and dropped a banner protesting rainforest destruction. It backfired. The action provided an excuse for the Malaysian government to crack down on national environmental groups like FOE-Malaysia. The government confiscated records, closed offices and even jailed activists to send them a warning—don't mess with our premier export commodity or we'll close you down.

In light of this situation, Yoke Ling suggested I visit Taman Nagara Park, a beautiful rainforest reserve in northern Malaysia. I think the last thing she wanted was someone from RAN, an organization known for civil disobedience with ties to Earth First! making any more waves. When I shared her recommendation with Randy, he shook his head and said, "Go to Sarawak." In his mind, tourists went to Taman Nagara Park and activists went to the Sarawak battlefront. It was being destroyed by Japanese companies like Mitsubishi and Marubeni Corporation. He left the decision to me, but I think he wanted me to see what rainforest destruction really looked like.

After the meetings ended, I headed to Kuala Lumpur, then to Penang, where Chinese, Indian, Native Malaysian, and Indonesian cultures converge. Exotic and culturally diverse, trishaws and bicyclists busily flooded the streets. I quickly learned the city had a darker side. As I strolled the streets, a Malaysian woman casually started talking to me. She invited me to lunch with her and a cousin, and I accepted. Of course I ended up paying for the meal, but for four dollars it was well worth the expense. She invited me to dinner with her family and offered to take me to a cool disco later that night. I told her to call at five o'clock and gave her my hotel and room number. She and her cousin walked me to the bus station. As they left, a slimy looking character came up to me and asked what that "Filipino girl" wanted from me. I hesitated, but told him she invited me to dinner and dancing afterward. He said she hung around this area a lot, worked as part of a syndicate that lured men into a "friendship," planted drugs on them, and then colluded with policemen to bust them. Now guilty of drug possession in Malaysia—a major offense—you could buy your way out of the problem for two thousand dollars. When he asked if I gave her the name of my hotel and room number, my face flushed. He suggested that I switch rooms immediately because "once the hook is set, the fish must be pulled in."

I thanked him and quickly flagged down a trishaw to go back to my hotel. As I was leaving the guy said to me, "I'll come over to your hotel in an hour to make sure you are okay." Sufficiently spooked by his story I said, "No thanks. I'm grateful for your help, but you've caused me to be extra cautious and I don't want *anyone* to come to my hotel." As the trishaw pedaled down the street, the driver asked what the guy said to me. I told him the story, and he told me the guy was conning me. He gets people's confidence and then tries to get money for his efforts. Who do you believe? So culturally naïve, I could easily have become a victim with the best of intentions. Maybe my trishaw driver was also lying to increase his tip. Needless to say I moved rooms and didn't answer the five o'clock call or go dancing. Did I avoid a frightening and expensive con game or did I offend a young woman with the best of intentions? Who knows?

I still had a decision to make. Do I buy a flight to Taman Nagara or Sarawak? Do I see beautiful pristine rainforests or clear-cuts and muddy rivers? I chose to fly to Kuching, East Malaysia, in Sarawak, Borneo. There I would decide whether to go any further into Sarawak or just do the tourist thing. In Kuching I could see a small protected piece of the rainforest called Baku Park, see a longhouse, take in the beach or shop for artifacts. Yet I knew it would be a wasted opportunity and frankly chicken shit not to go up the Rajang River into logging country. So I found an express boat schedule, checked a bag of clothes into the hotel storage room with all RAN identifying items, had a late dinner, decided not to call Laura and worry her with my decision, set the alarm for five in the morning, and tried to sleep.

Early the next morning, I got into an express boat that looked like a large cigar with windows, and we headed up the not-so-lazy Rajang River to Sibu, where I stayed the night. A relatively modern town by Sarawak standards, Sibu had no Westerners, so I attracted a lot of attention, especially in an old fashion movie theater showing *Terminator 2*. Now I probably should have wandered the city to take in the culture, but no, I did the Western thing. I went to a movie. In my defense, I wanted to see this movie and I thought seeing it in Sibu would make for a great memory. Maybe I was subconsciously looking for another white guy, even if he appeared on the movie screen. As I watched Arnold in the first major chase scene in an LA concrete river bed, I noticed that the people around me were watching me watching the movie. I think they wanted to see how I reacted.

Emboldened by *Terminator 2*, early the next morning I went down to the dock and bought a ticket to Belaga, where tourists have to register before being allowed to go further upstream. Six hours later, I was walking on its main "street," which consisted of a wooden plank sidewalk with earthy little storefronts beneath a row of upstairs "flats." I went into the first restaurant, ordered noodles (since there was no menu) and a handsome young man in his mid-twenties sat down at my table. He spoke English and introduced himself as Louis. He lived in a Kayan village upriver. A couple of cursory questions about where I was from and how long I planned to stay led to an offer to visit his longhouse. It was too easy.

It never occurred to me that I had a pocket full of Malaysian ringgit equivalent to four hundred US dollars, was being invited to visit a native village further upriver in what was once headhunter territory, and no one knew where I was in case I disappeared. Louis also suggested I not sign in at the government office, as they might decline my request to travel into logging country. I also didn't stop to think how this too meant there would be no record of my appearance in Belaga.

Louis wanted money to help pay for gas. He wanted much more than the actual price of the gas, but I decided we were both getting a good deal. He assured me that because of the recent rains the river would be high enough and the express boat would stop at his longhouse at 6:30 A.M. each morning so I would have no problem getting back downriver. I asked him to advise me on the gifts to bring, which is the custom in Sarawak. We went to the market and I bought sardines in chili sauce, brandy, a carton of Salem cigarettes, and biscuits for the kids. A slick path to the river took us to a small fiberglass boat with an outboard motor. As we took off

Up the Rajang

full speed upriver, we dodged floating limbs and trees—remnants of logging operations.

After half an hour we detoured up a muddy tributary to check his fishing nets, which stretched the full width of the river. Seeing nothing, Louis commented how the logging had made fishing much harder. We continued upriver and came to his longhouse. I loved the feeling of stepping barefooted onto the wooden walkway of the longhouse and washing mud off my feet. The spaciousness of his unit in the longhouse surprised me. Long cuts of red linoleum from the 1960s laid unattached over the hardwood floor. Ornate woven Asian round hats for working in the rice paddy hung on one wall. A picture of his father in Chieftain regalia, the former headman of the longhouse, hung on another. If he stayed, Louis would be the future headman. Another wall had a shelf with boat racing trophies. Every couple of years, all the longhouses on this stretch of the river had racing competitions. Obviously this village was the home of the top racers. Louis told me the long, hand-carved wooden boats they raced seated thirty-three men, with two abreast.

We walked into the large main room and Louis told me his father used to hold counsel there with the men of the community. He inherited this place when his father died four years prior. He had a wife and two children, and the whole family slept together in the bedroom. He also had a "slave" (I think he meant to say "servant")—a woman too old and weak to work and support herself, and treated somewhat like an outcast by the community. He took her into his house and she did anything he asked. She worked as nanny, backup cook, maid, and errand girl.

After touring the kitchen, which had cold water only and an open-air cooking "stove," the open-air bathroom and small storage room, Louis and I returned to the main room and talked for a while. Thankfully he spoke decent English. As we talked, I looked at the artwork, beadwork, ceremonial garments, woven baskets and animal skulls in this room. I asked Louis about his tattoo—an anchor with a serpent wrapped around it. He told me that men cannot wear tattoos unless they have proven themselves as hunters or warriors. The women, on the other hand, often have tattoos that look like sleeves, from the elbow down to the hand and then spreading across the tops of the fingers. They also have similar tattoos starting at the knees, going down to the feet and across the toes.

I asked Louis if it would be possible to go with him into the forest. To me that meant a nature walk. He interpreted that to mean a hunting trip. He said that he could arrange the trip, but he would have to rent the dogs from the headman. So as the twilight set in, we headed down the elevated riverside walkway of the longhouse catching glimpses of women preparing dinner and men in hammocks smoking pipes. We went into the headman's unit, made introductions with Louis translating, and then sat in a circle on the floor with the headman's family. One of the women sitting next to me prepared one of the Kayan's ceremonial offerings—the bitternut. She took a leaf and spread white ground up snail shell paste on it. She folded the leaf, wrapped it around a half-inch section of the bitternut, and placed it in a small lid in the center of the circle. As we talked, people picked up the wrapped bitternut and chewed it, so I did the same.

As the juices rolled down my throat, my face slowly started to flush, and my body started to sweat. I was having a hard time keeping my attention on Louis as he translated the headman's questions for me. The flame of the candle in the middle of the floor blurred, sending rays of light out in every direction. Then I felt the one thing you don't want to feel—a sphincter spasm. In hushed tones, I told Louis I needed to go to the bathroom—now. I tightened my anus and tried to make a graceful but rapid exit. Just in time. In the next five minutes my entire intestines were cleaned out.

Later in the evening, a few older men who worked for Louis stopped by to check me out (and the brandy I had brought). We sat on Louis' living room floor, drinking into the night. I asked questions, Louis translated to them, they answered, and Louis translated back to me. Eventually I asked them how they felt about the companies that logged the nearby forest. They said they were once wealthy. They had no money, but they had everything they could ever want: fruit, monkeys, deer, fish, all in abundance. Now they had to hike many miles to hunt. The companies had cut down many fruit trees, and the fish were small because logging operations eroded the soil which muddied the Rajang. I learned a lot, and it haunted me.

They all stood up together later that night, formed a line, began to chant, and performed a traditional line dance for me. Watching those older men doing simple but ancient moves together entranced me. At their request and a bit drunk, I stood up and started humming "Dancing in the Dark" by Bruce Springsteen, and did a disco skank with abandon. They were clearly entertained.

Before I went to bed on a small thin mat with a sheet, I showered under a near-full moon and stars, pouring lukewarm spring water over my head onto my body. It was refreshing like no shower I had ever felt before. The high pitched chirping of a hundred thousand cicadas filled the indigo night air. I looked at the forest behind me, relishing my luck and payoff for my courage. The thought of an All-American boy from Spokane, Washington, in a Kayan longhouse in Borneo thrilled me. And it felt so natural. Baptized into a new consciousness, I connected to an ancient part of myself that night, and it felt powerful and pure.

The next morning Louis made final arrangements with the headman for our hunting trip. We left with the headman, who came along to keep track of me. The dogs ran ahead, and after walking a short distance into the forest they started barking. Louis took off, and I stayed with the headman who would make occasional monkey calls. When he heard a reply or the dogs in the distance, we would move on slowly toward the sound. Soon the path ended and the headman took out his machete and began hacking away at the foliage. I had visions of African explorers in old Tarzan movies. We walked down into little valleys and then up little hillsides via the streambeds of rocks. We caught up with Louis who had already been far up the hillside and returned after seeing nothing. He had been making monkey calls in response to the headman's monkey calls. All along I thought we were hot on the trail of an amorous monkey. Turns out it was just Louis. We sat for a while and then heard the dogs bark again in the distance. Louis took off.

About thirty minutes later we heard a shotgun blast. Ten minutes later another shot went off. After another twenty minutes of bushwhacking, we met up with Louis again. He asked if we heard the shots and said he saw a moss deer near the paddy. He had fired once and wounded it, then tracked it through the jungle, found it again and made a clean shot to the throat. He told me I brought him luck; it was unusual to shoot a moss deer so close to the longhouse.

Louis and tribal elder in post hunting ritual

I took pictures of Louis with his deer. He was so proud and dressed it while I watched. One difference struck me. Louis saved every part of that deer. He even kept the stomach and the intestines; he turned them inside out and emptied the contents into the stream. We would eat these organs in soup later that night. He pulled out the kidneys and lungs last. While he finished the cleaning, the old headman began collecting wood for a small fire. He carefully shaved off little pieces for kindling. Louis gathered large fern leaves and made a mat on the ground. He stuck a stick through the two kidneys and lungs and rested it on the makeshift grill the headman had made.

We lit a small fire and cooked the deer organs. With a sharp stick, Louis poked the lungs until all the juices ran out. He pulled out a small sack of green rock salt and chilies, added a little water to them, cut the meat into small pieces and laid them on the plate of bright green leaves. Feeling slightly hypnotized, this seemed like a hunter's ritual to me.

We packed up the deer, walked home, and the headman carved it up. Then he divided the cuts into small piles. I sat quietly on the wooden walkway in the background, watching a mellow micro-market scene. Community women came over, talked as the meat was weighed and cut up, put in their orders, wrapped and paid for their portion. Later that afternoon, Louis gave me my share of the earnings from the sales of the deer meat—four dollars in ringgits. The best money I ever made.

Afterward we went back to Louis' unit. I wanted to take some photos and asked if he would walk around with me so people might be more willing to be photographed. He agreed to let me take pictures, but only on the condition that I promised to send copies of the pictures. He said that previous visitors had made the promise before, so he put himself on the line and asked people to pose, but the pictures never came. It pissed me off to think people wouldn't fulfill such a simple promise.

As we walked around, a playful air permeated as some people posed and others shied away from posing. Louis' "slave" posed for me. She put on an imitation gold-plated necklace with a cheap but pretty pink stone and stood without smiling for the picture. Given her status, I wondered if this was her most valued possession, how she acquired it and what it meant to her—questions too inappropriate to ask and best left unanswered. I quietly hoped that my request to photograph her had made her feel more than a slave, if just for a moment. I promised each of them I would send their picture, and wondered what they would think when they finally saw themselves.

Picture time ended when the headman came to get us. He needed every man to help carry a new $4,800 diesel generator from an express boat to the longhouse. Twenty-three guys (including me) made a strenuous climb up the sloping bank and set the generator in place. Everyone gathered around it; electricity had finally come to the longhouse! Now lights would replace candles at night.

Tribal men hauling the new diesel generator

I recorded the moment on film, but couldn't help thinking that some of the intimacy of late night candlelit conversations would be lost for future visitors. I questioned whether this milestone represented a positive leap forward in their 25,000 years of cultural evolution.

Before I went to sleep that night, I went out on the front veranda of the longhouse where wisps of clouds in the night sky floated past a full moon. The forest played a symphony of music. My trip was ending and I felt like crying. How could such a short visit feel so full and transformative? I felt proud and gratified that I had pressed on for an adventure up the Rajang and into the jungle where I experienced the beauty, sadness, and uncertainty of an ancient culture forced into modernity.

I felt such affection for these people and clearly saw how logging was destroying their ability to survive. I thought about how Louis said the biggest problems facing the longhouse started when the Japanese timber companies cut down the trees in their forest. In addition to the animals leaving, erosion made fish of any size disappear. The need to make more money to replace the fish and animals in their diet posed another big problem. For the next generation it meant facing the culture shock that comes from moving to the city and starting at the bottom of the economic pecking order.

They also faced the problem of protecting their land guarantees. The timber companies intentionally knocked down the wooden marker sticks that demarcate the community's property—its "land guarantee." Without the sticks they can't prove it's their land, so they have to survey again by paying a government person to come out, but that costs three hundred dollars. It could be even more expensive if several sticks are destroyed. They constantly struggled to retain their land rights and fight off the timber companies' encroachments on their tribal territories, or what was left of them.

I knew something that Louis might not have known. At the time, Malaysia's Prime Minister, Mahathir bin Mohamad, was aggressively trying to establish Malaysia as a high tech manufacturing center. To raise the capital he needed to build infrastructure in the cities to attract the Intels of the world, he needed to liquidate the one thing that could be converted into cash quickly—forests. Borneo has some of the most biodiverse rainforests in the world and some of the most unique creatures anywhere, but biodiversity doesn't produce instant cash, so Mahathir sold timber concessions to Japanese trading companies like Mitsubishi, who paid the locals shit wages to do dangerous work and ultimately to log themselves and their communities out of a living.

Under the full moon that night, I wondered about the inevitability of all of this. Western culture and its conveniences allure countries like Malaysia. Cities need to consume resources to produce jobs to generate income to fuel more consumption. They need electricity to power their conveniences. The needs of city dwellers lead their national governments to dam the rivers, displacing the natives and making it more difficult for them to survive, so they move to the city, find a job, buy their appliances, and perpetuate the destruction of thousands of years of their own culture and environment. How can this cycle be stopped? With the world population continuing to explode, it just keeps picking up speed. On my last night I forced myself to put this reality aside and instead feel enveloped by the ephemeral beauty of the moment.

A final good-bye at the dock

Early the next morning, I walked down to the dock with Louis. He heard the express boat coming from upriver, waved a white towel, and the boat approached the dock. One of the old men came down from the longhouse and stood with us. I almost started to cry when I said good-bye to Louis. He and the longhouse community had given me a gift I could never repay and would never forget.

I choked up as I climbed on board the cigar boat and took a last picture of them on the dock. We waved good-bye again as the boat pulled away. Homeward bound, I stared out the window of the air conditioned boat with a TV blaring an American wrestling show. I had told Louis I would try to come back, but never did. I did send him the pictures, and I know he got them because he wrote me back expressing his thanks for keeping my promise.

Up the Rajang

This trip up the Rajang changed the course of my life. When I got home I talked with Laura, then Randy, and decided to become an environmental activist. I took the Director of the International Boycott Mitsubishi Campaign position at RAN, which would become one of the largest international corporate environmental campaigns ever waged.

Dick Recchia of Mitsubishi Motors of America gave me this book, circa 1993. Permission of Penguin Random House Books, Inc.

The Roaring Fork River as Ally

When I took over the leadership of the International Boycott Mitsubishi Campaign at Rainforest Action Network (RAN), we immediately focused our efforts on Mitsubishi Motors' dealerships across the country. Our strategy entailed getting dozens of our Rainforest Action Groups (RAGs) across the country to hold banners saying "Mitsubishi Destroys Rainforests" in front of the dealership entrances during prime sales time on weekends. Fearful of losing sales, representatives put pressure on managers, who put pressure on the dealership owners, who put pressure on Dick Recchia, Senior Vice President of Operations for the US subsidiary of Mitsubishi Motors. Within a few weeks he requested a meeting at RAN.

Life as a River

Accompanied by Bill Shireman, his environmental consultant, in the meeting Dick claimed that Mitsubishi Motors had no power over Mitsubishi Corporation. He could do nothing. Being the self-designated "bad cop" for the meeting, I offered something he could do. "You can run a full-page ad in the *Asahi Shimbun* (Japan's *New York Times*) calling on Mitsubishi Corporation to stop destroying rainforests." To which he replied, "I could never do that." "Well when you can, let me know and we'll talk about not targeting your company," I responded. That effectively ended our first meeting.

I learned later from Bill that on the flight back he tried to calm an angry Dick down by saying, "Michael is just your typical environmentalist doing his job." Recchia retorted, "He's no typical environmentalist. Did you see those shoes?" I bought my Bally dress shoes in a moment of extravagance for $250 in 1988 when I worked as a management consultant. I made sure to wear them for this meeting knowing that CEOs recognize quality clothing and form judgements accordingly. I wanted him to take us seriously. And my Ballys helped him do just that.

I followed up the meeting with research on Recchia. One article mentioned that he loved fly fishing. A few months later I met with Shireman, who had been hired by Mitsubishi Motors and Electric to try and mediate a solution, and I casually mentioned that Dick and I shared a love of fly fishing. Any mediator worth their fee would jump all over this factoid and Shireman did exactly that. After Shireman returned from a fact-finding trip to Malaysia that supported our claims about the Mitsubishi Corporation's logging practices, he scheduled a second meeting with Dick and RAN. Bill coached us on starting the meeting in traditional Japanese fashion. Dick gave me a book entitled, *Trout: An Illustrated History*. I gave him an encased artificial golden stonefly and offered to take him down the Deschutes during the annual hatch. Every fly fisher knows the Deschutes is famous for its stonefly hatch. While the Bally shoes had elevated my status in his eyes, being a fly fisher took it to new heights.

Nearly two years into the campaign, Mitsubishi Corporation sent a representative to the US. I naively thought he would try to negotiate a resolution to the campaign. Instead he came to convince the American companies that Mitsubishi Corporation's logging operations were sustainable and our campaign was not seriously trying to find an acceptable solution. The first round of negotiations with the three Mitsubishi companies garnered nothing. So before the second round of negotiations, I met with Shireman and Recchia. In that meeting, we laid the foundation for a negotiation strategy where Mitsubishi Motors, Mitsubishi Electric and Mitsubishi Corporation would share the costs of an independent report on the sustainability of the Mitsubishi Corporation's rainforest operations. In exchange, we would stop all civil disobedience aimed at their companies while the research was conducted.

A couple of weeks before our second negotiation session at Rocky Mountain Institute's headquarters in Snowmass, Colorado, Dick Recchia called me. He had hired a fishing guide from the local Orvis shop in Basalt and invited me to spend the day before the negotiations on the Roaring Fork River with him. Suspicious of his ploy, but confident of the opportunity, I accepted his invitation.

Early in the morning on a chilly, sunny, late fall day, we met at the fly shop. Within an hour we waded into the Roaring Fork River. I was used to fishing the Deschutes River, which most fly fishers consider big water. Late fall on the Roaring Fork means low volume and lots of pocket water. This river didn't look like it held many fish, but I wasn't paying and this wasn't entirely about fish anyway.

It didn't take long to see that Dick was a rookie and not afraid to acknowledge it. When we came to the first good spot, he invited me to take the lead. I graciously declined the offer. Taking Dick's line, the guide tied on tippet and a size 16 caddis for an indicator and then tied one of his special nymph patterns to an eighteen-inch dropper attached to the caddis fly's shank. Following the guide's instructions, Dick approached the pocket water from the downside, casted his flies just above and let them drift through the hole. A second after the nymph hit the pocket a nice Brown trout was on. He howled with delight and fought him downstream as I moved in to repeat the tactic. BANG! Same thing. I rotated out to land my fish and Dick rotated in. This went on for the rest of the day as we methodically moved upriver.

Whenever we approached perfect holding water, I always made sure Dick went first. I knew he would appreciate the gesture. I might have played the role of bad cop when we first met, but that was business. This was fun...and business. On the river, one's true nature exposes itself. Are you competitive? Can you pitch shit on yourself when you screw up? Are you generous, patient, and careful with the fish? On the river that day, I realized that Recchia was a genuinely good guy who could be trusted. I think he saw the same in me.

By the end of the day we had each caught over thirty fish. So much for my initial evaluation of the river. Recchia paid the guide and tipped him handsomely. He exuded a youthful giddiness from having caught that many fish. I felt giddy myself. We sat at the bar next to the fly shop and ordered a couple of beers. By the time we were done drinking, we had agreed on two things. We had had a great day of fishing by any standard, and if Mitsubishi Corporation didn't agree to pay for the independent assessment of its logging operations, his company would. As expected, the next day Mitsubishi Corporation refused the deal. True to his word, together with Tachi Kiuchi, CEO of Mitsubishi Electric of America, Recchia split from Mitsubishi Corporation and agreed to pay for the independent assessment. And true to my word, we never engaged in civil disobedience after that when targeting these two companies. As agreed, however, our activists did continue to demonstrate; they just got more creative about how they did it.

Three years later, RAN did a side deal with Mitsubishi Motors and Electric that exempted them from the boycott. I flew down to meet with Dick and his senior staff to talk about implementation. During the trip we met with the company's "Earth Angels," a team of employees dedicated to finding ways to make the company more environmentally friendly in its day-to-day operations. When Dick introduced me, he beamed, referring to me as a "friend," though he admitted to his employees that it didn't start out that way. I felt the same way about him.

That day on the Roaring Fork helped turn the tide in the campaign. It taught me that even in battle always look for a way to connect with your opponent as a person. Find something in common. For business executives, the golf course has served as the classic venue for these kinds of relationship-based negotiations. For environmentalists, it seems appropriate that a river would provide the venue. Mother Nature can serve as a great ally when one negotiates on her behalf.

In later years I learned that getting corporate opponents into the woods, on rivers, in planes to see miles of clearcuts and talking to native peoples to show them the consequences of unsustainable logging practices often worked better than anything else to win them over. Seeing how their unsustainable practices affect nature and communities makes it difficult for them to remain in denial and resistant to change.

In 1998, Mitsubishi Corporation downgraded the timber division and began selling off its logging operations. Directors from that division no longer rose to senior executive positions. Imports from foreign operations declined significantly. A few years later, Minoru Makihara, the CEO of Mitsubishi Corporation during our campaign, would commit the company to obtaining independent certification of all of its remaining operations around the world. Along with Bill Shireman, Tachi Kiuchi coauthored the book called, *What We Learned in the Rainforest: Business Lessons from Nature*, and he joined Shireman to start Future500, a nonprofit dedicated to facilitating stakeholder engagement on corporate sustainability. Dick Recchia, upon retiring, started a website that sold high end fly fishing equipment mostly imported from Europe. That led to an invitation to be the location consultant for the ESPN2 series "In Search of Fly Water," which took him to fly fishing bucket list destinations like Mongolia, Seychelles, Brazil, and New Zealand. Eventually he landed in Redding, California, where he became president of the Shasta Trinity Fly Fishers. Who would have guessed?

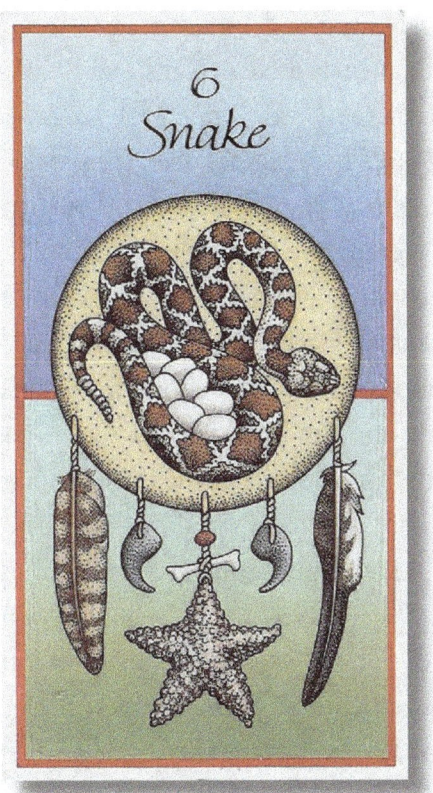

The Snake Card, from the Medicine Cards, by Jamie Sands, David Carson, and Angela C. Werneke (Illustrator)

Snake Medicine

For many years I've appreciated the work of psychologist, Carl Jung. He took Freud's theory of psychology into a spiritual direction with the concept of the "collective unconscious." When faced with a problem or challenge, signs or symbols can help us explore the collective unconscious for guidance. If we keep a keen eye out for signs or symbols and know their meaning, we can gain insight into the answer, solution, or direction to follow.

In the 1990s, Laura and I often tapped into one collection of symbols for guidance as a New Year's Eve ritual. We used a set of cards called Medicine Cards, which are based on Native American stories and lore. The original deck consists of forty-four cards, each one representing the medicine of a particular animal, bird, or insect. An accompanying book provides information on the meaning of drawing a particular card. Like most tribal peoples, Native Americans held pagan and animalist beliefs, including the idea that all beings in nature embody a certain energy or spirit. When that being appears to us at particular times, it is bringing a message from the Great Spirit or the tribe's ancestors.

For our annual Medicine Card ritual, Laura and I would ask the question, "What animal spirit do I need to guide me through the coming year?" Then each of us would draw a medicine card. On New Year's Eve in 1994, I drew a provocative card for 1995—the Snake. Its medicine signifies a time of transmutation when one sheds his or her skin, integrates male and female, and makes changes in attitudes and behavior. The card acts as a sign to go to the next level of consciousness.

This card came as I was ending my third year as the Director of the Boycott Mitsubishi Campaign for the Rainforest Action Network (RAN). Not only the largest corporation in the world at the time, Mitsubishi was also one of the world's worst corporate destroyers of forests. As the most prominent corporate environmental campaign in the US, the boycott had produced lots of demonstrations and civil disobedience at dealerships, auto shows, and electronics stores around the world. The Snake brought to mind that with all of its professional success, my personal life was suffering from my absorption in the campaign.

In the ensuing year, a big change happened. On Memorial Day weekend, Laura and I packed up our car with my grandfather's deer antlers sticking out of its sun roof and headed for our usual three-month stay at our 1930s home in Oregon. It sat on three acres split by a river called Clear Creek at the base of Mount Hood in a little town called Rhododendron. As the summer was coming to an end, we entertained the idea of staying a little longer that year. When September arrived we decided not to return to San Francisco as we had in the past. This decision began the shedding of my city skin for one of the woods.

While living in Rhododendron, I shed my international corporate campaign skin for local community activism. I prepared to pass the reins of the Mitsubishi Campaign to my assistant director. Living in the woods helped me shed other skin too, like the competitive keep-up-with-the-Joneses social comparison syndrome that permeated our social and professional lives in San Francisco. At the end of that year, I decided to leave RAN as an employee but stay on in a volunteer advisory role. I needed a break. I started doing trial consulting again. With members of our community, I helped found a small nonprofit called the Mount Hood Stewardship Council. Life started to feel more in balance.

At the end of the year, we drew Medicine Cards for 1996, and to my surprise I drew the Snake again, but this time in the contrary position (upside down). According to the Medicine Cards, drawing Snake in the contrary position means "…you may fear changing your present state of affairs because this may entail a short passage into discomfort. Does this discomfort keep you from assuming the viewpoint of the magician within? Is the old pattern safe, reliable, and a rut?" It advises to … "move through the dreamlike illusion that has insisted on static continuity, and find a new rhythm as your body glides across the sands of consciousness, like a river winding its way toward the great waters of the sea." Honestly, I wasn't exactly sure what this meant.

To learn more about what aspect of my life I needed to transmute, I drew another card—the Grouse in contrary position. It symbolized, "the sacred spiral…one of the oldest symbols of personal power…a metaphor for personal vision and enlightenment." Grouse "…symbolizes a lost connection to the Source…" and advises us to do the Grouse dance to once again become connected to Mother Earth.

Over the next several months, I realized I had worked as a warrior for the Earth and now I needed to more fully embrace the Earth's spirit. A richer meaning of life revealed itself as I deepened my relationship with the natural world. I also felt more meaning as I deepened my relationship with myself, my relationship with Laura, our land in Oregon, fly fishing, playing guitar, singing, reading, photography, my close friends, and work. During this time, I also began working out in the gym and encountered an older body builder. He talked to me about deeper muscle workouts to strengthen the muscles around my heart so they could support my passions. It made me wonder how many "teachers" would come to me if only I had the courage to ask for guidance and the wisdom to listen without judgment.

That summer something happened that made me think I wouldn't draw Snake again on New Year's Eve. Paul Franklin, another friend, and I rendezvoused for a day of fishing at Dry Creek near Warm Springs, the main town on the Warm Springs Reservation. While we were having lunch before hiking downriver, a beat-up van with three inebriated Indian male teenagers passed by us. With rock and roll blaring and in a cloud of dust they stopped near the restroom. I have to admit that I get a little nervous when drunk Indians show up. Despite the fact they make money off non-Indians who pay a fee to fish their side of the river, decades of understandable resentment bubble beneath the surface for some of them when they see us on their land. Does that stop us? No. The fishing is too good there. It just makes us a little more cautious about which car we drive and what we leave in it.

As typical male teenagers do, they laughed, had playful banter, punched each other, kept the radio blasting, and drank more beer. They became enthralled with something on the ground near the restroom. They circled it, threw rocks at it, shot staples from a gun, and jabbed it with a stick. All the while they were laughing, drinking, and giving each other shit. Then one of the boys found a broken limb and picked up the victim of their harassment—a three-foot-long snake. I couldn't tell whether it was dead or alive, but I knew it couldn't be doing well after their rapacious ritual. He held the snake up by its tail, grabbed the staple gun from one of his friends, and walked to the restroom. The teen affixed the snake to the door with its tail up and head down, with thirty staples running the length of its body. Then he stepped back, surveyed and approved his brutal artistry, picked up his beer, walked back to the van with his buddies and drove off leaving another cloud of dust and fading heavy metal rock and roll in the air.

The three of us watched from about a hundred feet away. My friends just shook their heads in disgust and returned to eating lunch. I felt sick. I couldn't stand seeing that snake nailed to the wall. I pulled out a screwdriver and pliers from a little toolkit in the trunk of my car and walked to the restroom. I couldn't believe this cruel scene; a beautiful nonpoisonous bull snake hanging on an outhouse, flattened in spots by staples, ripped by rocks, head crushed. As tears welled up, I used the screwdriver and pliers to take out every staple, one by one. As I pulled out the last one, I held the snake's tail so it wouldn't fall to the ground.

I knew this snake needed to return to the Earth. I draped it over my arm and walked out into the mowed golden cheatgrass.

Still holding its tail, I slowly lowered the snake head first to the ground, forming a spiral with its body. I crouched down, held my hand over the snake and said a prayer for Mother Earth to take its spirit home. I hoped that by leaving it where a hawk could see it, the snake's body would become food for a bird of prey and its spirit would soar to the heavens. I walked back to join my friends who had watched the whole ritual. In the past being so sentimental and expressive in this way would have made me embarrassed, but that day it didn't even occur to me to care about what they thought.

The next Friday I drove back to Warm Springs. I like to camp at Mecca Flats on warm summer nights. It sits across and upriver from the Dry Creek Campground. I fixed myself pasta on my ancient Coleman stove, opened a bottle of wine, lit a candle and had dinner just as the sun was setting. I washed my dishes in the river, sat back in my folding lounge chair, and took a couple of hits of pot. The rim rock glowed, the Deschutes' surface water shimmered, and the moon rose over the canyon wall.

I woke up early to a warm morning and hiked down the well-worn path along the river, knowing that several guys had already covered this ground and were wading into my favorite spots farther downriver. Feeling a slight breeze, I came to the section of river directly across from last week's scene at Dry Creek. Not thinking about that ordeal, I saw a ghostly iridescent snake skin, gently draped over metallic green sage brush and blowing slightly in the breeze. So delicate from head to tail, it had only a few small tears in the skin and looked in perfect condition. I could see the finest details of its body preserved in the skin—even its eyes. As I stared at this piece of natural art I heard the words, "This is a gift from snake. You have shed your skin."

I don't remember if I caught a fish that day, but I do remember that I hid the skin, picked it up on the way home, and found a

Snake Medicine

Snake skin from Mecca Flats

way to preserve it between two pieces of glass in a thin metal frame. This snake skin remains one of the most precious gifts I've ever been given. It has sat on my desk at work ever since as a reminder of why I do what I do.

I didn't draw Snake that New Year's Eve and haven't drawn it since. I'm sure it will reappear one day when I need it. One thing for sure, since that day on Dry Creek, I've never seen a snake the same way.

My turn at the oars of our fourteen-foot inflatable raft on the Rogue, 2010

"Mike Marx Is Dead"

A few weeks before taking our annual Rogue River whitewater rafting trip with my band of Oregon brothers I had a frightening dream. In a raft on the Rogue River, we approached the tough Class V rapid, Blossom Bar. As we entered the rapid we came to Picket Fence, which consists of three huge partially submerged boulders standing side by side. Getting through Blossom Bar requires rowing straight toward Picket as you enter the rapid and then pulling hard toward mid-stream at the last minute. In the dream, this didn't happen; at Picket Fence we capsized.

Two years before having this nightmare, my buddy Jeff Wiles miraculously rowed us through Picket in high water—and in a drift boat. No one is supposed to go through the Picket Fence with a drift boat and come out the other side…at least not with the boat. It hit the only possible seam perfectly, kicked up, tilted sideways, dove down the other side and filled completely with water, but we were able to get ourselves downriver without capsizing. We've never lived that down with our river brothers.

In my dream we were rafting in an inflatable raft and didn't pull off toward mid-stream in time. The raft hit the boulders, turned and rolled up on its side, and flipped over backward. Wiles and I were thrown under the raft. The immense water pressure pushed me down a rock chute. Forced through an ever-shrinking tube, I got trapped. I let go and gave in to my fate. Yet something gave way. I somehow shot through an opening and up to the surface.

I wrestled with the intense current, made my way to the rock bank, and climbed along a rock wall to where the raft sat pinned against the huge boulders that make up the "fence" of Picket Fence. I didn't see Wiles. With no time to lose, I harnessed myself to a rope line and the guys held it as I dove down after Wiles. I wondered whether I'd find him, let alone free him. Then the dream ended, probably before both of us drowned.

A few weeks later when we were rafting the Rogue, for a frightening few seconds I thought my dream was about to come true. I had just rowed three of us through Blossom Bar without incident. I felt greatly relieved. We rested with everyone else below Blossom, celebrated our success, and then pulled back onto the river. A bit later we stopped for lunch across from Paradise Lodge. After lunch our buddy Yates wanted to row the raft for a while. While not an experienced oarsman, Wiles and I knew that from here on out we'd encounter light water with small rapids, so Yates took the oars. Relaxed, sunning, drinking beer and talking, Wiles and I sat up in the bow—without life jackets on.

We approached a bend in the river where the water jams up against the rock embankment, swirls around to the left and back into the mainstream. Maybe a Class I in a normal year, it turns out this wasn't a normal year and we were acting way too casual. Wiles and I were enjoying the scene when all of a sudden in front of us we saw a submerged tree snag sticking two feet out of the water. Too late for Yates to pull us away from danger in high water, Wiles barely got his life jacket on, and I got one arm into a jacket before the water pushed the left side of the raft onto the snag as the right side went under water.

The strong current flipped the raft over backward and threw us out. I went under the raft. So did Wiles. I held tightly to the life jacket and was trying to feel my way under the raft when it got caught on something. I feared if I let go of the life jacket I would be swept by the current under the snag or possibly under the river bank. I had no choice. Out of breath and with the life jacket not budging, I realized I was about to live my dream.

I let go, got my feet out in front of me so I wouldn't hit my head, and was swept by the rushing force of current around the river's bend to the rock wall. I surfaced, frantically swam with the current, and angled my way toward shore. I swam into a calmer back eddy and grabbed the downriver side of the rock wall. I looked upstream and saw Yates swimming behind me. I yelled, "Is Wiles out?" He hollered back, "I think so. I saw his head come up."

"Think so" definitely did not comfort me. I climbed up on the rock wall and saw Wiles' lower body wedged between our overturned and submerged raft and another one that hung on the snag like a Dali sculpture on a dead tree. Next to him an inflatable Tahiti wrapped around the snag. We were obviously not the first to bite it here.

It took thirty minutes and help from a gutsy young guy who watched the whole episode from a kayak further up river to get the raft and Wiles off the snag. Shaken, I thought—what if there had been just the slightest variation in the configuration of the raft, the snag or the rock wall? I could have been trapped and drowned. Earlier as we stood on the rock cliffs above Blossom Bar, I remembered saying to Wiles that I didn't fear rapids like this one because I knew myself well enough to know that I would more likely die in a moment of inattentiveness than going through a challenging rapid. That moment of inattentiveness had just happened.

When we finally caught up with the other rafts, Wiles and Yates went up to join the circle and tell the story. It took me about thirty minutes of organizing the raft and setting clothes and sleeping bags out to dry before I was ready to join the others. I needed that time for a bit of post-traumatic stress reduction.

I didn't have much to say when I joined them. I tried to put on my cool face and manner, but my friends saw "seriously spooked" all over my face. After dinner, my buddy Dan Neal pulled out his guitar and entertained us as usual. After a few songs from the standard repertoire to which I failed to sing harmonies with my usual engagement, he went impromptu with a song that refrained with, "Mike Marx is Dead." Only a thirty-year friend with a great sense of humor and a brilliant knack for improvising songs could have pulled it off. It was hilarious. His song put everything in perspective. We were alive, had an adventure, could laugh and sing about it, and had a story to tell for years to come. And one thing for sure, we all would be wearing life jackets on the river from now on.

The Green River below the Flaming Gorge Dam, 2004

The Odyssey: Utah, Wyoming, and Idaho in a Week

One summer my good buddy Kirk got a wild idea for a fishing trip he called, "The Odyssey." He convinced Wayne and me to give the workaholics in us a break and hit the road for a week of serious fishing on amazing rivers in Utah, Wyoming and Idaho. Kirk launched the voyage solo from San Diego with his Ford Explorer loaded with camping and fishing gear, bags of his favorite chips, a cooler of Coronas, and Johnny Cash's latest CD, "The Man Comes Around" playing in an infinite loop. He picked me up at the Salt Lake City airport after spending a long night in Vegas, and we set course for the Green River.

Day 1: Green River below Flaming Gorge Dam

Kirk had fished the Green River below the Flaming Gorge Dam once before. On the way there he regaled me with stories about fishing with imitation red ants and having to take the oars when his guide found himself embarrassingly alone on the bank as his boat and client headed downstream. Kirk alleged the Green River supported eleven thousand fish per mile in this section of the river. Whether a "story" or true, his claim gave credence to his insistence that fishing the Green was a "must."

With high expectations for a twenty-plus fish day, in the morning we met up with our guide at the put in. Pat, a former dentist who chucked it all to guide and fish, immediately previewed the day's reality. "It'll be tough fishing today but you should have a chance to touch fifteen fish." Wait a minute. Up to eleven thousand fish per mile on an eight-mile float? By my calculation that potentially comes to eighty-eight thousand fish we're floating over! In guide talk, saying fifteen fish usually means landing five to seven fish. Suddenly the Green didn't sound like the "must" fishing destination to me. Still, you know the bumper sticker: "Any day fishing is better than a day working."

Pat advised us to prepare to wade wet, so I wore shorts, something I never do and will never do again. What a mistake. Slathering on 45 SPF sunblock only deluded me into thinking my pasty white thighs were protected. Two hours downriver and already feeling the heat of a sun burn, I borrowed extra t-shirts from Kirk and Pat and wrapped them around my legs. Not exactly sporting the look of fly fisher sartorial chic, I insisted all pictures must be of fish and above the waist.

After missing numerous lightning fast takes and eventually landing a few nice Cutthroats and Browns, the clouds started to roll in and we pulled over for lunch under a huge Ponderosa Pine.

The Odyssey: Utah, Wyoming, and Idaho in a Week

Just as Pat laid out a spread of the Colonel's famous deep fried chicken, potato salad, and Coke, a standard afternoon weather pattern descended upon us. Thunder exploded in the distance and flashes of lightning lit up the sky. Within minutes, big dark black clouds let loose a torrent of huge raindrops, more lightning and ear shattering bursts of thunder, making that huge Ponderosa Pine a dubious shelter in the storm.

As it commonly happens in these high elevation environs, the storm passed almost as fast as it came. We packed up lunch and resumed the float downriver, casting ourselves silly. On rivers like the Deschutes it is illegal to cast from a boat, so when it's legal you appreciate those long, boat-aided natural drifts close to the bank. Our percentages went up post-lunch. The most memorable moment occurred when Kirk casted his fly and the top section of the rod went flying down his fly line into the river. At that exact moment a beautiful eighteen-inch Brown took the fly. Panicked that if he broke off the fish he would lose his rod, Kirk fought it brilliantly with the remaining butt section of his rod. It ended up being the biggest fish of the day and the best story.

When we hit the last mile of the drift, the aftermath of the downpour finally caught up to us. The river roiled red from the erosion of clay soil, but we fished it anyway with little or no action. By the end of the day, though, I bet each of us touched twenty fish and landed about half of them. We called that a good day, although one landed trout for every eight thousand we floated over isn't exactly what I'd call "good."

Kirk's Brown trout on the Green River

True to the spirit of an odyssey we packed up, set out in the Ford Explorer, and let the winds take us where they would. A couple of hours later we landed at a great resort restaurant near Pinedale, a small Wyoming town populated by farmers, ranchers, and a few fishers. Unfortunately, the resort was full and it looked like we might be camping under the stars until a lovely young waitress overheard our plight and offered us her room. She would stay with a friend. When does that happen? Appropriately, we watched the movie *American Beauty* on Kirk's laptop before crashing.

Day 2: The Upper Green River

Before heading out to our next random fishing destination, we did the usual stop at a fly shop to get a little advice. The guide recommended Green River north of town, and of course fifty dollars' worth of "must have" flies.

After the Warren Bridge, we drove up a dirt access road north of Pinedale and entered BLM land. We followed it up the river and checked things out. It looked like an exceptional high mountain fly fishing river. Riffles, runs, and big boulders said "trout everywhere." Unfortunately, we weren't told that fishers can do more than fly fish this section of the Green. They can kill fish with bait and spinners all day, which people obviously did. Farmers and ranchers tend to be pretty pragmatic about catching fish and putting them to good use. By late summer, the fish population drops dramatically, and the remnant survivors have become very smart.

We unpacked, geared up, and waded in near a great camp site on a ridge. With hoppers and monstrous Chernobyl Ants as the flies de jour, I had the hot hand and managed to land a few, the biggest at about fourteen inches. Kirk got a lot of hits but found it more frustrating, so he broke off early to cook dinner for us.

That evening we had a quintessential summer camping scene. Despite fighting a twenty-mile per-hour wind with gusts even higher, Kirk prepared a salmon dinner that rivaled any meal we had in restaurants on the trip with the possible exception of the one made by Jenny Lake Lodge's five-star chef. After dinner, he crawled into the tent, turned on his headlamp and read. With a chorus of cicadas providing "sense-a-round sound," I pulled out the nylon string guitar he had brought, tuned it, and fumbled through my limited Dylan and Springsteen repertoire. At about eleven o'clock, a full moon came up over the hillside and sent a magical oscillating stream of reflecting gold dust on the slow-moving Green.

I wish we could have camped a couple more nights there. We owned the place. No one interfered with our water during the day or interrupted its quietude at night. The whole scene had a way of emotionally grounding me. Calming and soothing, the scene reminded me of one of the reasons I love this sport. Through quiet moments of reflection in nature you can touch your soul and find peace.

Early the next morning I hit five or six fish on a Royal Coachman. The river had big boulders and pocket water, but most of the fish swam in the riffles and deeper runs just after the riffles. By around ten o'clock or so things slowed down. Kirk broke down camp, and we moved on to Jackson Hole.

Day 3: Flat Creek

After a stunning drive along Highway 191, we arrived in Jackson and checked in at the Jack Dennis Fly Shop to confirm our guided trip on the Snake the next day. The Old West vibe of the town lured us into the Cowboy Bar for lunch. We found it hard to resist sitting at the bar on saddle stools, but a quick test said, "You ain't gonna like this!"

Post lunch we headed a mile or so north of town to Flat Creek, which runs down the middle of an elk preserve meadow on the edge of town. After dawning waders and boots and rigging up our rods, we stupidly hiked what seemed like a mile in the wrong direction. However, our blunder rewarded us with spotting intact skeletons of three elk. It looked as if they had lain down and died together. The bones weren't even scattered as you would expect with coyotes or wolves around. That probably was because they died amidst thousands of elk gathered for the winter in Jackson's Elk Preserve where they have safety in numbers and the elders can die in peace. Still, seeing three intact skeletons lying there so serenely felt a little eerie, as if we had stumbled into a sacred burial ground.

When we finally fished, we didn't catch many, but those we did catch measured much bigger than I expected. The trout tended to school up in the river bends and the first fisher there got the action. Unlike me, Kirk figured out Flat Creek fairly quickly. A natural caster from early on, it helped that he casted with the only red hopper we had. It helped even more that he could gently drop the fly onto the slowly meandering gin-clear stream without spooking the fish. Of course, casting a 4-weight rod didn't hurt his presentation either. I watched him and thought maybe one day I'll refine the perfect casting technique for this kind of river.

The panoramic painting of that meadow hangs prominently in my mental gallery. Surrounded by towering mountains, Flat Creek meanders through long, flat, and narrow moist grasslands. It flows through the meadow with a reticence of a stream that knows it is coming to the end, about to transform into a marsh and slowly disappear below ground.

We learned later that starting in late October, between five and seven thousand elk come down from the mountains of the Grand Tetons, Yellowstone, and Gros Ventre to winter here. The community augments their diet with hay. The Boy Scouts collect their shed antlers, sell them to local businesses, and then donate the money to pay for the hay. Perfect symbiosis.

Since it was mid-August, we didn't see any live elk in the preserve, but we did see them later that night after we picked up Wayne at the airport. When we drove into the Teton National Park to eat dinner at the Jenny Lake Lodge, we saw an impressive sight, and a first for me—about seventy big, beautiful elk in a single herd.

Impressive also captures the dinner that followed. With a famous chef and five-star rating, the restaurant lived up to its billing. Every single bite of our five course meal was delicious. This lodge may look humble compared to Timberline, Crater Lake or Ahwahnee Lodge standards, but the food definitely ranked superior. Our meal there won the culinary award of the trip.

Day 4: The Snake River

Sammy and Kirk on the Snake River

The next morning we met our guide, Sammy, at the Jack Dennis Fly Shop in Jackson. Within an hour we were floating the Snake River. I'll never forget the scene. The surrounding Tetons rose like royalty over the valley and provided a stunning backdrop. Guide Sammy, a cranky, middle-aged bachelor mountain man with an edge, worked hard to put us into fish. One catch that day stands out in my memory. I saw a trout sipping flies under a tree near a bank and made a long cast. Nothing. Sammy pulled us back upstream and I casted again hooking into and landing a beautiful fine spotted Cutthroat. I love the look of this distinctive and picturesque fish. In my opinion, only big brown Redsides that inhabit the Deschutes and mature brookies rival it.

Later, we beached the boat and Sammy told Kirk to fish the riffle upriver. As the more experienced fisher, he told me to "go explore." I did and found a series of small riffle-fed pools formed by water that temporarily broke off from the main river channel. I got down on all fours and snuck up on the area in classic *Curtis Creek Manifesto* style. Once in position, I took a moment to think carefully about my impending cast. Then I gently tossed the fly into the top of the riffle and sure enough…BANG! A pretty fifteen-inch Cutthroat took it, and I landed him. After a few futile casts, I moved downstream and repeated the drama. BANG! The element of surprise delivered a second Cutthroat.

I doubt many fishers wandered off the Snake's main stem far enough to fish that little stretch. Doing so taught me a good lesson; don't just stay in the boat. Fish the tributaries or small off-shoot streams. Small water can produce fish, especially when fishers pass it over for bigger waters. To this day, we wax poetically about the numbers and size of the fish we caught on this float trip.

Day 5: The South Fork of the Snake

High from our previous day's experience on the Snake, we eagerly agreed to go thirty miles west of town and take on the South Fork of the Snake. Floating the South Fork of the Snake reminded me of one of the reasons I hate dams. Dam operators constantly raise and lower the water level, which has to throw off the fish. For ten thousand years, fish have been programmed to find their feeding position and stay there. Then dams get built to produce electricity, control floods and guarantee farmers irrigation water, which constantly messes with the water levels and makes fish aquatic neurotics.

The Odyssey: Utah, Wyoming, and Idaho in a Week

I know, the South Fork, like many tailwater fisheries, wouldn't offer the fishing it does if it didn't have cool clean water from a controlled release. I would trade all the good dam-created fishing opportunities to see these rivers run naturally the way they have for millennia. Then again, global warming may force me to change my opinion. Dammed rivers like the Snake will likely be our best fishing rivers for the next couple hundred years (assuming our species survives).

So dams giveth and dams taketh away. On day five of our Odyssey, this dam tooketh away. Definitely tweaked with high water flow, our guide did not oar well with four of us in his fiberglass drift boat. We should have never had that many people in a fiberglass boat on that river during high flow. The weather, fishing, optimism, and the interpersonal vibe all ran cold that day. Had the guide checked the water flows, he would have known to go somewhere else, like back to the upper section of the Snake.

At one point it felt like we were careening down the river canyon and bypassing all the best spots. And indeed we were. Then in the middle of the river, Wayne hooked what seemed like a big trout. Normally in this situation a guide would slow the boat down and provide counsel on how to land the fish. But ours didn't have enough control of the boat, so Kirk and I shouted advice, "Let him run, hand off the reel until he stops, reel quickly, keep your tip up, strip-strip-strip." Wayne dragged that fish downriver for what seemed like half a mile before he finally landed a gorgeous twenty-inch Cutthroat. Being new to the game, I don't think Wayne quite realized the significance of catching this fish. That night at dinner, when Kirk pointed to a mounted Cutthroat of similar size on the restaurant wall, Wayne realized he had caught a mount-worthy fish!

Michael's Fine-Spotted Cutthroat trout

I also had a memorable moment later that day. We had pulled ashore to give our exhausted guide a rest. I walked up a shallow slow moving tributary where I spotted three large Cutthroats sipping flies off the surface in a diverted back channel pool just below a riffle. I made a long cast of a Rusty Spinner below the riffle and let it drift slowly down to where the fish were working. A slow take, the prick of the hook and the fish exploded, bee-lining it for the weeds. I managed to slow him down just before he could become entangled. I played him carefully, knowing he had been fooled by a size 20 dry fly with a pinched barb that could easily come unbuttoned. At the end of the fight a picture perfect yellow-orange-brown fine spotted Cutthroat slid into my outreached net.

These moments remind me that spotting, casting to, hooking and landing big fish on little dry flies damn near hits the experiential apex of fly fishing. We may have seen little action that day and encountered lots of annoyances, but that one fish made it forever memorable for me. For an entirely different reason, catching nothing but a white sucker made it memorable for Kirk. And losing his fly fishing virginity with a near trophy Cutthroat made it memorable for Wayne. Three guys. One boat. Same river. Terrible action. Three distinctly memorable experiences.

I tell myself that days like this play an inevitable and important part of the overall experience of fishing. They make the good days on a river, the good guides, and the prolific catching all the more special. It's trite, but true. Like in the rest of life, we need contrast in fishing. To have the full experience we need big rivers and the small ones. We catch big fish and small fish. We get dry fly action and nymphing action. We deal with harsh weather and welcome perfect cloud covered Pale Morning Dun days. We have generous fishing buddies who give us the best holes, their secret fly, or front seat in the boat, and we experience selfish, competitive fishers we'll never fish with again.

I continue to strive to know myself and my sport well enough to maximize the good aspects and minimize the bad. I know the bad aspects will always happen because fly fishing is grounded in nature and nature is inherently unpredictable, which makes the sport all the more interesting and challenging.

Day 6: Cascade Canyon above Jenny Lake

A wild native Brook trout in Cascade Canyon

Over breakfast, Kirk, Wayne and I discussed plans for our last day. Wayne and I were flying out of Idaho Falls that night and Kirk was driving his vessel to home port. I recall that Kirk and Wayne were hell-bent on one last day on a river whereas I could have taken a long beautiful hike. They remember just the opposite. Two memories against one suggest I had to get one last fix. And it turned out to be arguably the best day of the Odyssey.

We dressed light, rigged up our 4-weight rods, packed water bottles and cameras and headed off around Jenny Lake. I saw a picture perfect stream running into the lake and made a quick cast that produced a little four-inch brookie and then nothing else. Forget it, we got back on the path and headed for Cascade Canyon at a brisk pace. Below the falls the river had fishing potential, but Kirk decided to push on above the falls. I would have stayed low. Kirk occasionally pushes me into situations I wouldn't experience—fortunately. As we hiked up toward the canyon, we jokingly fantasized of a meandering river chock-full of fish, with Bonnie Raitt and Susan Sarandon there (both on my Top Ten list), sunbathing nude.

Another mile up the canyon we came to enticing little riffles and pools. Trout heaven. I stayed, and of course Kirk headed up the river farther. I caught about fifteen little eight to ten-inch brookies on hoppers. Then I headed up the path and saw Kirk was fishing beaver dam tailwaters that winded across the canyon floor. There he hit probably the biggest fish in the river—a few ten to twelve-inch brookies.

But the climax of the day happened as he was rounding the bend of the river. He looked straight across the twenty-foot wide channel and saw two huge dark moose lying in tall vivid green weeds by the river. They were looking straight at him. Kirk wisely decided that he could leave the next stretch to other fishers... and the moose. We named them Bonnie and Susan, added them to our list of incredible birds and beasts we'd spotted on this trip, and headed back to the car. That day we hiked seven miles, fished an hour, caught a bunch of the prettiest fish, and saw Bonnie and Susan in all their shape-shifted glory. Although we weren't sure how to explain their antlers.

You get these kind of days after the South Fork days if you keep perspective, have a sense of humor and go for the whole experience instead of just big fish. Taking all of it in means witnessing the gestalt of scenes like a perfect riffle that becomes a pool that reflects amazing cumulus clouds in relief against the softest blue sky as a four-point buck emerges from behind a two-hundred-year-old cedar to take a drink. Ultimately, taking it all in means deeply revering the art created by four billion years of evolution.

The Odyssey: Utah, Wyoming, and Idaho in a Week

As we headed down the path from the canyon and picked up the one bordering the lake, we saw a Flaming Gorge cap propped up on a post. A synchronistic farewell sign, it triggered flashbacks from an amazing week. As we headed to the airport, Kirk played the official Odyssey CD by Johnny Cash. Talk about a guy who lived the contrasts of good and bad and survived to tell the story with gritty musical wisdom. Listening to him reminds me to relish once-in-a-lifetime experiences like this one.

A pod of six humpback whales cruising together in a remote inlet in northern British Columbia, 2002

Raised by Whales

I enjoy making and remaking my "Ten Best Lists." I have my ten favorite movies, ten favorite female actors, ten favorite albums of all time and of course, my ten best days fishing. The fishing list includes the morning I hooked five and landed three steelhead on the Salmon River, the twenty-plus fish day during the stonefly hatch on the Deschutes above Warm Springs, and the twenty-plus fish day on Slough Creek.

I also have a Top Ten Nature experience list. A whale watching trip in British Columbia will always remain on this list. It permanently burned into my mind the dignity, power and intelligence of these massive and ancient creatures.

In 2002, I was working as the cofounder and executive director of the nonprofit, ForestEthics, which strove to protect the last ancient temperate rainforest of British Columbia (BC) and the native communities that live there. After a two-year battle and an agreement with the British Columbia government and three major timber companies, we were in the process of forming working partnerships with First Nations on the coast of the Great Bear Rainforest to help them transition to ecologically sustainable economies. We were engaged in a grand experiment designed to wean native communities off their forced dependence on logging jobs and revenues and back onto a more marine and conservation-based economy. My BC staff had been negotiating protocols that would guide our partnership and it was now time for the "chief" of ForestEthics to meet with the chiefs of the Haida, Kitasoo, and Heltsuik Nations.

My closest friend and board member Jeff Wiles flew with me to Prince Rupert, and we met up with Merran Smith and a couple other ForestEthics' Canadian staff. One tough activist, Merran and two other women in their late thirties successfully negotiated a deal with three male CEOs of the largest forest products companies on the BC coast to protect over five million acres of the most sensitive and pristine temperate rainforest valleys in North America. I was looking forward to in-person time with her. We thought we'd be flying out shortly for Haida Gwaii to meet with the Haida Chief, Guujaaw. No such luck. On the BC coast you can make your flight plans, but more often than not, Mother Nature decides if and when you fly. We holed up at a local brew pub and waited for the fog to clear enough to get out. After several hours and beers, we decided to forget the flight and take an overnight ferry to Haida Gwaii. Since it left around 9:30 P.M., we had time to kill, so we got the idea to take a whale watching excursion, something I'd never done before.

Eight of us loaded onto a thirty-foot aluminum tour boat and cruised for about an hour up the coast. I honestly didn't expect to see whales any more than I expected to see grizzlies. Guide comments like these characterize my prior experiences of trips like this: "You should have been here yesterday." "You won't believe what happened the next day after we dropped you off." So when we entered an inlet and approached the mouth of the river and our guide spotted a pod of six humpback whales cruising the coastline, I was thrilled. My luck had turned.

The guide pulled in about a hundred feet from the whales and tailed them until they dove out of sight. The six whales disappeared from the surface just about the time I got my camera out of the bag, focused, and prepared to shoot. I thought I had missed the opportunity but the guide said to watch the surface for boils. We watched for a couple of minutes. Next thing I know about a hundred yards from us all six whales came out of the water in a perfect circle. We shrieked in awe of their wide open mouths, heads the size of Volkswagens, all in a tight thirty-foot-diameter circle. They were fishing for herring by diving down to the ocean floor, forming up and releasing thousands of little bubbles that created a circular casing that "trapped" the herring inside. Then they rose together through the funnel they had created, mouths sucking in everything that didn't escape. The guide said they needed to consume about a ton and a half of krill, small crustaceans, and small fish every day to survive. I took this to mean that we might see an encore performance...and we did.

As we tailed the whales for about forty-five minutes, they dove and surfaced four times. One of them breached off in the distance before forming up again with the pod. They dove and headed toward the river's mouth. I figured they were just covering ground, but in retrospect, they may have been luring our privacy-invading tour boat into a narrower channel where the river entered the inlet. I remember saying to Merran that it feels like we are too close; we're invading their space. I wanted to say something to the guide, but it didn't seem appropriate to tell him how to do his business. He seemed knowledgeable, and besides, how often do you get this close to six humpback whales?

We drove up the river's mouth, and the current looked fairly strong. The captain idled the boat at a low speed just to stay in place. Like most coastal inlets, there was no shore on which to land a boat. The shoreline was eroded by the river's current and the tides so that if you tried to go ashore in low tide (which this was), you would quickly see that "land" is eight feet above the water and overhangs a concave wall of rocks. The whole scene looked very unforgiving.

The whales dove again in the river's mouth. We sat about seventy-five feet away from them, and I thought this would be the perfect opportunity to get a picture. Camera in hand, I climbed up on the roof of the boat. Despite a slick metal surface and no guard rail, the roof positioned me for a perfect shot. I set the camera shutter speed for fast action, and Merran and I excitedly scanned the river for boils for several minutes.

"My God!" cried Merran. I looked down and saw hundreds of little fish leaping out of the water all around the boat. Then she shouted, "Oh my God!" The boiling water suddenly exploded as this huge black monstrous mouth rose out of the depths right next to the port side gunnel of the boat. Its fully extended jaws were full of water, and in total amazement we looked right into its mouth.

Then I realized that the boat was rising straight up out of the water. As Merran and I fell to the floor of the roof, our one-ton metal craft rocked to starboard like a toy boat. A second whale came up under the bow. The boat tilted sharply to the side and I saw a third and fourth whale right next to the starboard gunnel. Another came up under the stern, and still another came up directly under the boat. Together the whales had lifted the boat completely out of water!

These huge whales raised us up nearly six feet off the surface and then let us drop. The boat hit the water, rocked back to port, and sent a ripple of waves in all directions. Hearts in our mouths we all looked at each other wide-eyed and shaking. "Wow!" In the shock of it all, we nervously chattered about how close we came to swimming, or worse, going Jonah-in-the-whale. We wondered aloud what would happen if we had fallen into a whale's mouth. We wanted to believe it would cough us up, but I'm sure I wasn't the only one imagining being inside a whale's cavernous stomach with no way out alive.

Rightfully shaken, our guide (and we) knew he had tailed the pod too closely. We all wondered if these brilliant forces of nature had decided to give us a thrill and a warning. We got the point. The guide pulled the boat two hundred yards away from the pod. He feared that the whale that hit the stern might have cut itself on the propeller. He felt horrible and had us worried. What irony if a bunch of enviros were responsible for injuring or killing one of Mother Earth's most astounding creatures! We were greatly relieved when we saw all six whales rise again off in the distance. Fifteen minutes later, four of the whales did full breaches one after the other. Unbelievable! It was as if they were saying, "We'll give you a show, but keep your distance or else…"

Now near sunset, we headed home to catch the ferry. As the curtain of fog lifted, we watched a huge yellow-orange ball rolling slowly off the edge of the ocean's horizon. It created a spectacular array of pinkish orange lit clouds with a royal blue backdrop. I got my picture, not of the whales breaching, but of the sun sinking. To this day it remains one of my favorite sunset pictures because of what preceded it. I wish I had captured the whales breaching, but I think some images are just meant for memory alone.

Life as a River

Sunset on the Pacific off the BC coast

I am convinced those whales knew exactly what they were doing. Rising around and under the boat was no accident. They meant to lift us out of the water to scare us, not hurt us. These whales gave me one of the greatest gifts in my life. Being raised by them always brings to mind a line from a Springsteen song, "You can look, but you better not touch, boy."

The valley through which "The River That Cannot Be Named" runs hidden by the riparian, 2017.

The River That Cannot Be Named

Jeff, Kirk, Wayne and I went on quite a number of annual eight-day fishing trips. This particular year we had fished in Yellowstone for three days and were looking to day four. So far the catching fell below average compared to previous years. Thunder showers every afternoon didn't help. On one of the days a huge lightning storm completely blew out the Lamar and turned it into a milk chocolate-colored rampaging torrent.

On day four, we exited the East Gate of Yellowstone. Shortly after we exited the park, we stopped to check out a river we hoped to fish and picked up sandwiches for later. We walked over to a bridge and looked down into a shallow canyon to witness a completely unfishable stream, the result of another major thunderstorm in its headwaters. We decided to have lunch and check the map for other possible rivers outside this blown-out watershed.

While eating lunch at a picnic table, a father and son from Oklahoma walked by and interrupted our map analysis. They had fished the little stream that paralleled the road we traveled that morning out of the park. Unaffected by the rain, it joined the muddy river we had nixed just below the bridge. Too small and right along the road, we didn't even consider it a possibility. We couldn't even find its name on the Yellowstone Park map. The father said they caught a few little guys and he had hooked into a big one just up from the bridge. Out of options except blowing off the day and heading to Cody, we decided, what the hell. Let's drive back upriver, split up and fish it.

Jeff and I drove back into the park and stopped at a pull out high above the stream. It looked like nice water. Geared up, I backtracked down the highway about a quarter of a mile. I looked over the highway railing to see a high and steep shale bank. It looked like the kind of river entry that few would dare, so of course I went over the guard rail and slowly (except when I slid out of control) "boot skied" my way down the steep slope. At the river's edge I tied on an ant imitation and scanned the water upstream. On the left, the mountain came almost to the streambank. On the right, a thin strip of standing and downed trees discouraged thoughts of walking the bank, leaving wading the stream the best option, although stretches of darker water suggested even wading might be tricky at points.

I started moving upstream, casting as I went. Nothing. Pretty much what I expected, but at least I was wading in a river with anticipation instead of in a car feeling like I just wasted a precious vacation afternoon. It started raining hard. I approached fast moving water rushing over rocks and under trees with trunks bending out over the stream and saw an unexplainable cable tightly connecting one bank to the other. I snuck up slowly on the run from the right and made a low cast to miss the cable. My ant landed just below the riffle that fed the run near the tree. I watched it drift almost the entire ten-foot run when out from the bank beneath the tree I caught a pale shadow streaking toward the fly. With no hesitation, a beautiful wild native Cutthroat trout took the fly and dove as I set the hook. Its trip back to the tree interrupted, it streaked upstream, leaped out of the water, dove, leaped again and headed downstream with me clumsily in pursuit, sliding over boulders mid-stream as I tried to hold the rod tip steady. Despite being in shock at what I had hooked into and the unartful chase that followed, I managed to bring him to the net. Wow! I've seen plenty of seventeen-inch wild, native Fine-Spotted Cutthroat trout, but unexpectedly seeing one in a creek like this made it all the more stunningly beautiful.

Moving a bit upstream, I hit another Cutthroat almost the same size. A little farther upstream, I hit another one, then another one. All of them measured in the fifteen to seventeen-inch range. As I approached where we parked the car, I spotted Jeff in the distance. It looked as if he had only moved a few yards at most from where he first waded into the river. I yelled over to him, "How'd you do?" He yelled back, "Maybe the best hour of fly fishing in my life!" What? He said he had caught eight beautiful Cutthroats and large Rainbows. "What were you using?" I asked in disbelief. "A dry, but they were taking the nymph dropper nearly every time." Nymphs? I thought the creek seemed too small for a nymph dropper, but learning Jeff used it I realized I had another option beyond the dry. I waved to him and headed downstream again with a dropper in my future tactical plans.

This time I went farther downriver to hit some fresh water. After a long butt slide down the shale embankment, I tied on a small Prince Nymph dropper to a hopper imitation, cast it upstream against the far granite wall and was immediately jerked into a new reality by what turned out to be a beautiful nineteen-inch Rainbow trout. After landing it and a couple of smaller ones, I doubled back on my previous route upstream. Over the course of the next hour, I landed another four to five large Rainbows and Cutthroats. I caught the bows on the nymph, the cuts on the dry.

When Jeff and I joined up again, we had one of those fisher conversations in which most of the sentences start with: "Can you believe…" or "No one's going to believe us when we tell them…" When Kirk and Wayne finally rejoined us, the same giddy conversation ensued, as they too were shocked by the action.

That afternoon on that creek would rank as the most unexpected great afternoon of fly fishing ever if a day on "The River That Cannot Be Named" in the Big Horn Mountains (Hint #1) hadn't followed a few days later. It cannot be named because my brothers would kill me, but you'll get some hints.

Jeff and Wayne flew home after we fished the Big Horn River out of Thermopolis, Wyoming. Kirk and I pumped our guides for some tips on how to spend our last two days. Guides can be pretty generous with their tips after we proved generous with ours. One of our guides suggested we try "The River That Cannot Be Named." We said that we had already fished that river earlier on this trip and described the section. He replied, "Yeah, that's a good stretch of water, but the only section I fish is further up below the beaver dams" (Hint #2). Hmm.

When we fished this same river two years earlier, we were pleasantly surprised by the number and size of the native, wild Cutthroat we landed. We found a meadow higher upriver than where all the other fishers' rigs were parked. A herd of fifty or so cows grazed at the top of the meadow, which partially explains why the fishing wasn't even better. Grazing cows mean minimally healthy riparian, soft muddy banks, and of course cow piss. Trout loathe holding where cows constantly wade in. Not only do they piss on them, the cows destroy their perfect lies.

Earlier in the trip we stopped fishing about a mile below the area the guide recommended because the water ran skinny. So small, I would be amazed if the river ran fifty cubic feet per second in this section (Hint #3). As it turns out, however, a combination of factors makes this section of the river incredibly good fishing. First, it gets less pressure because you have to be in decent shape to hike down to it and back out again (Hint #4). Second, fishers pass it by because they can't see the great holding water from the road due to the high brush and riparian. Third, smaller than the earlier unnamed creek in this story, it runs like a stream. It couldn't possibly hold big fish!

Clear, cold water that snakes down a narrow valley also makes this river so stellar. A hundred feet of riparian on each side comprised of dense, eight- to ten-foot-tall bushes protect the stream (Hint #5). Each time it bends, the river feeds into deeper holding water that protects fish with the depth and darkness of the water and the roots shooting down through the embankment into the stream below. Not so surprisingly big fish hold under the cut banks behind the protective roots. And because of the water quality and thick riparian, caddis, mayflies, and terrestrials thrive.

Kirk and I drove upriver to where we spotted the beaver dam. While not huge, the beavers had built a minor engineering feat. The shallow elevated pool covered half the meadow. A curved earthen dam of mud and sticks on the lower end held it in place, and as we would discover later, had enough strength to support a fisher looking for a less hazardous route out of the canyon and back up to the road.

We drove back down about half mile and parked. Given the river size, I pulled out my very first fly rod—a nine-foot 4-weight, slow action, thirty-year-old Scott. It would make fighting smaller fish more exciting. We chose our respective sections and I took off over the hill to the back of the canyon meadow where mine began. After I bushwhacked my way through the tangled web of thin trunks and branches, I came to the small river. I could see spots where fish might hold. The voice of the young boy inside me said, "Ooooh, fun! No risk. No big casts. Sneak up on them. Quick battles and lots of little guys. Glad I brought my 4-weight." Then the old man in me kicked in and scanned the hillside above to make sure it's bear-free, put his hand reassuringly on the bear spray attached to my belt, and sent a high-pitched "aaaaah-ooooo" to avoid surprising these large unfriendly creatures.

At six thousand feet elevation, the partially cloudy day felt cool enough to justify a light rain jacket and warm enough to trigger a series of bug hatches. With one scan of the river, I could see flitting and floating of caddis and mayflies above the water. I chose a caddis and attached it to 5X tippet. As I expected, the initial straight stretch of water with its shallow but chaotic current offered up a couple of decent cuts. As I waded upstream, the river moved toward mid-meadow and ran through a narrow corridor of saplings. I had to duck down almost to water level while wading mid-stream to get under the interwoven branches from each side of the stream. I came to a small opening, a bend in the river, and a quintessential pool running ten feet in length, fed by a shallow five-foot-wide chute and partially hidden by overhanging limbs thick with leaves.

I paused and watched the water for a few minutes. Soon I saw a small disturbance on the surface, a little higher in the run. I focused more intensely on the surface for bugs. I saw nothing, but then the sun exposed a small mayfly rising gracefully off the water. The water moved slowly in this run so I put on 6X tippet and attached a small Parachute Adams, a perfect bug for a little twelve-inch fish.

I saw another rise, made a short cast into the chute, and within two seconds of it landing, a pretty fifteen-inch Cutthroat lazily took the fly. Bigger than I expected, it fought better than I expected. After landing it my expectations for this stream jumped. I waited a few minutes before casting again, this time six inches off the far bank. Another trout in the fifteen-inch range took it. A fire of excitement flared up inside. This could be one of those great days.

Some rivers you fish make you feel like a man. Like the upper section of Slough Creek in very slow water, casting thirty-plus feet to lazily rising fish where you have to perfectly employ years of practice and knowledge. Other rivers make you feel like an old man, like the Madison, Yellowstone, or Deschutes, which constantly remind you that you're slowly losing balance and leg strength as you age. Occasionally a river makes you feel like a kid again—like this one imbued with magic. This section of The River That Cannot Be Named poses no fear of drowning or even falling. Hidden by tall riparian, you feel like you've found a secret place where you alone get to play. It has willing fish that don't require a whole lot of technique, just a little bug knowledge and attention to detail. It has fish more decorative than almost any animal in nature and bigger than a little stream like this would justify. And most of all, youthful anticipation makes you wonder if an even bigger fish lurks around the next turn.

For the next hour every time I came to a bend and pool, I would fool at least one decent-sized fish. Wading to my next corner hole, I looked up and watched a rather large s-shaped fly slowly rising overhead, then another. It took me a few seconds to realize I was seeing gray instead of Green Drakes; they can be different colors on different rivers. I picked up my pace and found a fishable stretch nearby. Not knowing how picky these fish would be, I put on a black-winged Green Drake dry. It had rested undisturbed in my fly box for years and would have to do.

I remember thinking, "I've always wanted to fish a Green Drake hatch." Guides talk about it as if it ranks right up there with the salmon and stonefly hatches, or the October caddis hatch. I had one brief shot at a drake hatch on the Fall River in Oregon a couple of years earlier with Jeff. A big Rainbow on the far bank attacked my fly with such ferocity that it bent my rod in half and broke me off. I had put on an emerger imitation, but I didn't change the tippet from 5X to something stronger like 3X. With my permission Jeff then casted a Green Drake dry fly to the same fish, and this time the fish did not escape. That fish dwarfed everything else we landed that day.

Shaking with anticipation, I studied the water and made one cast to the tail-out of the pool near the undercut bank. Bam! The Green Drake heralded as the fly of the moment! Within two seconds of taking that fly, this big, strong fish turned and with lightning speed muscled his way back under the cut bank. I could feel its head shake, but as hard as I pulled he didn't give an inch. I moved the tip of the rod to different positions thinking I could pull him from behind a root. I tightened, then relaxed the line, and tightened it again from a different angle. Nothing. Given the 5X tippet I forgot to change, it was only a matter of time before my line betrayed me.

I hate leaving a fly in a fish! Even though research shows the fly will become dislodged or dissolved in a matter of days, I still hate it. Pissed at myself, I changed to 4X tippet. Of course that's all I brought because why would I need 3X tippet on such a tiny river and a 4-weight rod? I put on another Green Drake dry fly—my last one. I caught a nice cutty with it higher in that run, did a better job of controlling the fight, landed him, felt reassured, and then moved upstream to the next corner hole with the hatch still in motion.

The scene looked almost the same as before. Ready this time, on the opposite bank I saw the tail of a large fish waving gracefully below subsurface branches at the back of the run. I tightened my drag a little for more control and surveyed the river beside and below me. I casted upstream of the fish and watched its tail disappear. That fish crushed the fly, dove, felt the hook's sting and leaped two feet off the shallow streambed. As he leaped I lifted the rod high in the air to take out the slack while stripping line with my left hand as fast as I could. He splashed down like a rock and despite my tighter drag, stronger tippet, and knowledge of exactly what he would do, he streaked back to the tangle of roots. Within seconds he probably wrapped the line around two or three of them. I momentarily hoped I could pull him free, but when I pulled so did he and the line-wrapped branches gave him enough leverage to send my floating line limply back to me. Dammit! Another gorgeous cutty, my last dry dun imitation left in his mouth, and I had made the same damn mistake two times in a row.

Fortunately, I had four emerger patterns designed to sit on the surface like a tightly wrapped, curved exoskeleton waiting to free its wings. Like the dries, they had sat in my fly box for ten years. I thought they may not even float upright. I tied one on, greased it heavily, tightened the drag even more, and reminded myself that I was fishing with a slow action (meaning soft tip) 4-weight rod. I would have to be much more aggressive about pulling the fish to my side of the river and moving the fight downstream of me. I casted the new fly, and within a second it met a big splash and fierce yank. I made one big strip of the line, raised the rod tip, pointed it high up behind me, twisted my wrist to guide him downstream, and then stripped more line to prevent him from getting back across stream to safety.

Life as a River

A native Cutthoat trout caught on The River That Cannot Be Named

After a series of rapid-fire evasive maneuvers, I got him close enough to pull out my net and finish the battle. Which brings me to one of my pet issues in this sport—landing nets. Moments like this in rivers reinforce why I deal with the hassle of a landing net. Without one, you have to fight the fish longer to weaken it enough to grab or wedge it against the wet stones in order to dislodge the fly. Meanwhile, you've exhausted it, wiped off some of its thin protective mucus coating by bouncing it off the exposed rocks, squeezed and possibly damaged its inner organs, and risked it escaping before being revived. Okay, I'll get off the soap box, but use a net!

I fished that drake imitation for the next hour and repeated this scene over and over. I lost count of these gorgeous, wild, healthy Cutthroat fighters, but they all measured in the fourteen to eighteen-inch range. Although it was a small river, these fish fought hard and smart.

That day on The River That Cannot Be Named made me look at rivers a little differently. I began to think about the different river personalities. Some run with extraverted, domineering and brash qualities. Others feel more introverted, humble, and submissive. Some strike you as Type A—impatient, eager to get to their destination. Others seem in no hurry, savoring every twist and turn along the way. Some may feel old as they enter the sea, and others young as they rip fresh off a mountain. Some come off as all-work, others all-play.

The River That Cannot Be Named

This section of The River That Cannot Be Named falls into the category of young, secretive, naïve, virginal and full of surprises. It presents itself as mysterious yet willing to share its treasures once you enter its hidden world. It extends an earthy invitation to step back in time when as kids fishing felt like a complete novelty. It brings back the time when fishing awakened us to the dynamics of a river, the behavior of fish, the mechanics of a rod and reel, the colorful lures, salmon eggs and slimy worms. It returns us to a time when fishing provided a total escape from school, chores, parental discipline and the more arduous and sometimes psychologically painful experiences of everyday reality. For many of us, a river offered our first experience of a relationship with nature. The River That Cannot Be Named takes me back to when I learned that some of the best experiences in life lie beneath the surface, beyond our sight, if we're willing to believe and seek them out.

In Native American lore, the raven is revered as the intelligent trickster. I took this photo in 1999.

My Shamanic Journey

The whole concept and reality of Shamans fascinates me. In primitive societies Shamans' roles included being doctors, psychologists, priests, and channelers of the animal spirits. Societies that believed all living things have a spirit and that spirit would educate, protect, and sustain us revered Shamans. They thought Shamans could summon, communicate and translate spirit wisdom to us.

I had heard of people doing guided "spiritual journeys" with a Shaman and mentioned this one night in a spring equinox sweat at my friend Christy Slovacek's home in the woods near Mount Hood. An accomplished pianist, composer and artist, Christy also practiced shamanic journeying after studying for several years with a modern-day Shaman. Six weeks later, I was pulling into her driveway for a journey I would never forget.

Would it be a sweat? Would I take drugs? Would it involve meditation? As I wondered what to expect, Christy handed me a couple of heavy blankets and said, "Follow me." We walked to a cluster of old cedar trees on the banks of the Sandy River. She asked me what I wanted to know. I said I wanted information to help me answer, "What is my spiritual truth for now?" Five months earlier, I had left the Rainforest Action Network and had yet to figure out what was next in my environmental work.

Christy instructed me to sit down on some mossy boulders near the water's edge and focus all of my attention on the river and my question. She then walked into the nearby grove of cedars and performed a ceremony to call on the spirits from the four directions. When she finished the ceremony, Christy sat down near me, leaned back, put a blanket over her head, and journeyed on my behalf.

I found it challenging to sit there trying to meditate on the river and my journey's intention. I focused on my intention, and when my mind wandered I quickly came back to the question as I watched the freezing clear water of the Sandy performing an ever-changing aquatic dance. I became mesmerized by the rushing water's interaction with the sunlight and shadows. Half an hour passed, but it seemed much longer when Christy pulled the blanket from over her head, rose and gestured for me to join her at the top of the sloping river bank. Here's what she told me.

She held out the small turtle talisman I had given her to represent me during her journey. Turtle represents both feminine energy and Mother Earth. Christy said the turtle pulled her down through the water into a narrowing tunnel. As it pulled her deeper, the tunnel began to rise and she could see light from an opening above. When she broke through the surface she was in the midst of a large white flower. It looked very much like an exquisitely bright, soft and perfectly formed Calla Lily. A golden ball of nectar or pollen was rolling up the side of the flower. As it reached the upper edge of the blossom, she saw a second vision.

Christy saw me standing on a precipice or high place on a steep canyon wall. My arms outstretched upward and my palms opened to the sky as if calling upon some divine energy. Laura stood across the canyon on a similarly steep mountainside. She too had arms outstretched. Far below us a river ran through the canyon. It was a river of blood. Suddenly a raven grabbed me by my shoulders, lifted me up and we flew across the deep chasm.

When the raven and I reached the mid-point of the chasm, I began dropping parts of myself that looked like undefinable objects into the river below. As these things fell away, I became lighter and transformed into the raven. I continued to fly until I reached Laura. I landed on her right shoulder. It seemed as though this position had symbolic significance to her.

As I sat on Laura's shoulder Christy had a third vision. She focused on the raven's shimmering golden eye. As she looked closer the colors around the pupil became more visible. Red. Brown. Green. The golden iris shone like the center circle of a huge stain glass window in a cathedral. She was being pulled through the pupil and emerged inside a large church. There I was, a boy being crowned king with a slender golden crown. She knew I felt emotionally torn. I had the capacity to lead but felt regretful of losing my childhood, creativity and playful abandon. An artistic side was being sacrificed to a higher calling, and I felt both sad and resigned to my duty.

Christy believed I lived as a boy king in Northern Britain, Ireland or Scotland in a former life. My struggle in this life involves passion. She said that the word "passion" had leaped out at her early and formed the theme for the entire journey. "Your life is about passion," she said. "Passion is your truth."

We continued sitting by the river and talked about the importance of a daily ritual. As we talked she remembered that the raven gave one last instruction at the end of the journey. I should walk down to Clear Creek, which flows through our property, and each day wash my face, hands, and chest with its water and allow its consciousness to enter and cleanse me. I believe in ritual and this instruction felt very natural to me. I resolved to follow her instruction starting the next day.

I left thinking that I needed to begin listening more to the feminine in and around me. Feminine energy is filled with generosity and wisdom. Laura helped me become more enlightened about the complexities of relationships. Sitting in her chair amidst the freshly tilled soil, my aging garden partner Linda taught me how to plant and cultivate a vegetable garden. My masseuse Karen taught me how massage can go beyond the physical and feel more like a spiritual experience. I also realized that I have been learning from women since my birth: my mother Vivian, my Grandma Holly, my sister Marie, and my first passionate love, Stephanie. The amazing women environmental activists I've worked with have also taught me a lifetime of lessons. Many women have infused me with a deep appreciation of the power of the feminine.

Sometimes I thought I was listening too much to the feminine and needed to increase the volume on the masculine in order to restore balance. Ultimately I concluded that the masculine cannot be fully itself without interacting with the feminine. The masculine takes on the challenge, and the feminine appreciates the value of process and partners with the masculine to achieve their purpose. Without the feminine, there is no masculine, and vice versa.

The morning after my journey I walked down to the bank of Clear Creek. Blue sky and cumulus clouds reflected in its glassy runs. I touched the cold water and then touched my forehead, my eyes, my lips, and my heart. I stood up on a large boulder, looked up at the great 250-year-old grandparent Douglas fir and hemlock trees across the stream, stretched out my arms and uplifted my palms to the sky. As I asked their spirits to guide me, I heard the croak of a raven downriver.

I held my pose and turned my head toward the sound. Fifty yards away and no more than twenty feet above the water a beautiful black raven glided into view and sailed upriver between its two tree-lined banks. It turned its head and looked down at me. Then it floated gracefully right by me and croaked again as it passed. I followed its flight in utter amazement as it continued effortlessly upstream leaving one last croak as an exclamation mark on the experience before disappearing around the river's bend. I stood there in stunned silence. Then I started to smile, shaking my head in disbelief. I never saw a raven make that flight before or since.

Experiences like this make me believe another dimension is operating that we can see, but only if we look through our own raven's eye. I now understand why the oldest religions have the central belief that all living things have a spirit and if we seek their guidance, they will give us instruction on how to circumnavigate life's obstacles in pursuit of our personal mission. I can't bear the thought of allowing the destruction of millennia of the natural word's benevolence and wisdom, and this fuels my passion for protecting it. We need all natural beings to realize our spiritual and human potential. In our relationship to the natural world lies the secret to our deeper selves and why we are here.

The biggest wild Rainbow trout I've ever landed, White River, Oregon
Photo by Hanalei Vierra, 2006

Fighting a Freight Train

When we lived in the woods of Rhododendron, Oregon, each morning I looked at my "fishing gallery" on my bathroom wall. It had pictures of all my fishing buddies. One picture in particular triggers a mental highlights reel every time I look at it. I'm holding an eight-pound, muscle bound Rainbow. It has a little sand on its snout and its gill plate shows a little red where it has not quite grown back from a previous injury—probably from a foul hookup with a fisher. Every time I see this picture, I recall asking myself, "If this was the biggest, hardest fighting trout I had ever landed, why didn't I take a little extra time to wash the sand off his face and turn him to the picture perfect, uninjured side?" Answer: These imperfections are part of the story of the most exciting fish I ever landed.

Playing guide to dear friends M'Lissa and Hanalei on the White River that day, I sure wanted to put them into fish. They had caught fish the day before in float tubes on high mountain desert lakes on the plateau just east of the Deschutes River. But the barren basalt hills and murky shallow lake aesthetic didn't appeal to them. They wanted to fish a river. Who could blame them? Lakes are beautiful, and fishers find man-made lakes fun, but the true aesthetic milieu of most fly fishers, even rookies, belongs to rivers. And these two rookies had a little Zen fisher in them, so their desire to change venues didn't surprise me. It suited me just fine.

We woke up early on a Sunday morning, packed up and headed toward my favorite private water in Oregon. John Justesen and his brother Fred own about five miles of White River, a Deschutes tributary. Often un-fishable, the fall and spring rains make it a roiling flow of milk chocolate with zero visibility. In the summer it becomes dirty powder white with about six-inch visibility due to the melting glacial silt of Mount Hood. It gets so bad that it blows out the Deschutes River for miles below its confluence.

Windows of opportunity do come, however, when the river is low, cold and relatively clear. This was one of them. A brisk fall day, the alders and maples were turning yellow, the ground was covered with an orange-brown carpet of dead leaves, and a slight misting of rain enveloped us. It took about an hour to get these rookies rigged up and outfitted in waders and boots. I took them to a spot where my buddy Kirk and I had caught large trout before.

A big logjam had formed from flooding the previous spring when the river had washed out the bridge connecting Mount Hood to the town of Hood River. The river had to have been another six feet higher to build this chaotic, impenetrable wall of logs strong enough to bend the river off course. After giving my pupils some instruction, I put M'Lissa in the prime water where a couple of years earlier Kirk's line unwound at such warp speed and went so far into the backing that his futile attempt to slow the beast by tightening the drag was all it took to set it free. I put Hanalei downriver a hundred feet from her in less productive water and stayed with him to help him cover it skillfully. They looked much happier fishing a river, whether they caught anything or not. So was I. Rivers just feel more challenging. Fly fishers have to learn to think like a river…or more accurately like a fish in a river.

M'Lissa had no known strikes, which surprised me. So I offered to take a couple of casts. I changed the nymph, and cast right where she had been repeatedly working the chute. Nymphs are the only way to fish the White River most of the time, which means you have to maintain concentration on that little yellow piece of Styrofoam, watching for a slight delay in the line. It took me years to learn I needed to react to every hesitation in the line because it likely meant a fish was tasting the bug.

I got a slight delay in the indicator and quickly raised the rod tip. With the fish on, I handed her the rod. She deftly fought and landed a nice sixteen-inch trout. Then we fished for about an hour working our way downstream. As it neared time to wrap things up and head back to our cabin, I instructed Hanalei to go back upstream about a hundred feet from where we began and work that stretch of the river. I had caught the biggest fish I ever caught in White River right there. A nice run goes under some trees with big submerged boulders and a rock wall along part of the opposite bank. You have to move slowly under the branches to avoid getting snagged and you have to cast side-arm.

When I joined Hanalei about ten minutes later, he had already worked his way up to the chute that starts the run. Having given Hanalei my rod, I had my buddy Jeff Wiles' funky old 5 to 6-weight and a borderline Scientific Angler reel that was way too small for the amount of line rolled onto it. I tied on a stonefly nymph with a very small pinkish-orange glow bug on a dropper. I've caught most of my fish in this river on little glow bugs. On this particular river I'm not an elitist who shuns the salmon egg imitation. However, every time I tie one of these colorful little balls of yarn, I get a little queasy about the fact that I'm not imitating a bug at all. I have to remind myself that this sport is about *imitations*, not necessarily about *bug imitations*, even if it's called "fly fishing." It's about fooling the fish.

I threw in a line while Hanalei continued to work the chute. I must have cast five times, each one another two feet further across the river. Nothing. I moved up a few feet and started again. My third cast landed mid-stream when my indicator stalled. I lifted the rod tip quickly and BAM! My line went zero to sixty in three seconds! I had hooked a freight train. My yellow floating line ripped right down the middle of the river so fast I could hear it cutting it in two. Thankfully I had set my drag tight knowing monsters lurked in this water. Fortunately, my stonefly nymph was tied to 3X tippet. Unfortunately, I had tied the dropper fly with 4X tippet, which was way too weak for a fish this powerful. Was he on the dropper or the stonefly? The drag worked to stop the fish short of the downstream chute, which if he had run through, based on Kirk's experience would mean I'd never see that fish.

Wiles' cheap rod bent into a half oval from the pressure. I needed a 6 to 7-weight rod for this fish. Suddenly the train switched directions going full speed back upstream. To keep the line taut, I started stripping faster than I've ever stripped a line in my life. As it passed me, it suddenly turned and without pause raced downstream again. The wet line burned through my fingers. Just as the fish approached the logjam, what looked like a steelhead jumped three feet out of the water. The strong sideways leap had Hanalei and me screaming a paraphrase of a line from Springsteen's song "Lost in the Flood," "Wow man! Did you see that? That fish hit the water with such a beautiful thud!" We were both whooping and hollering an octave above normal in two-part cacophony.

On the bank above me, Hanalei yelled, "Hold on to him!" After another quick run upstream, more stripping, followed by a dash into the current again, my quarry raced toward the logjam and then took the dreaded left turn through the chute. Its sprint upstream and down had drained some horsepower, but obviously I needed to get my ass moving downstream to stay up with this fish. Holding a steady pressure with concentration I have rarely been known to sustain, I stumbled awkwardly downstream over logs and boulders, climbing gingerly onto the giant logjam. It was easily six feet high and thirty feet wide. Just as I started to descend from it, I saw a beautiful huge silver Rainbow lie over on its side for a moment. Its size and depth left me awestruck and even more determined to land this monster. Hanalei's "Oh my God! Look at that fish!" stole the words right out of my mouth.

Once I traversed the logjam and waded an unexpectedly deep and powerful side stream, it was just a matter of horsing this stubborn giant into shore again and again until it finally succumbed to Hanalei's fourth attempt to net it. Wide-eyed, Hanalei stared at the fish and then looked at me and said, "I have seen a master in action!" Honestly, while I'm far from a master fly fisher, I sure felt like a master at that moment, and an ecstatic one at that. This was the most challenging fish I had ever fought and landed. Giddy like a little kid who had never caught a fish in his life, I looked at the fish and thought that despite the forty-foot falls a few miles downstream that made it an impossibility, it had to be a steelhead. It was too big and ferocious of a fighter not to be. My Native Trout Society friends confirmed later that my "steelhead" was instead an old, huge, muscle-bound trout, and seeing them was not that unusual in this private stretch of the river.

Hanalei got his camera and I took the fish out of the net. With an aggressive burst of energy, it freed itself from my grasp. Damn, if it didn't almost get away. We chased it on our knees into the shallows, and between the two of us and the net managed to get it back in our grasp. I kept it in the water while Hanalei readied his camera. I had to get this picture. So did he. When he gave the word, I lifted this strong, wide and deep trout and realized it had to weigh eight pounds! Hanalei got the shot.

We had put this fish through enough. I quickly lowered him into the water, held him for about sixty seconds in the freezing glacier-fed river and was prepared to hold him until my hands went numb, but a strong move said it was revived and safe to let it go. With the resolve of a defeated prizefighter who would return again to the ring for another bout it expected to win, it swam back into the murky green shadowy depths of the river and disappeared.

A high-five with Hanalei, a thanks for the great support he lent during the battle, a few moments of the fight recounted, and it was time to pick up the net and head home. We looked around for the net. Nothing. Now losing a net in a small river seems impossible to me. I especially hate to lose an expensive hand-made laminated oblong wooden framed version with the expensive fabric netting. We looked everywhere. Gone. I walked the bank downstream a few yards. I eyed several places where it should have gotten snagged. No sign of it anywhere. Unbelievable! I had just caught the biggest and toughest fish in my life and it cost me the most expensive net I ever owned in my life.

What's that about? Something in my Catholic boy upbringing said, "It's your offering in return for this incredible experience." Something's gained, something's lost. Every pleasure exacts a price. When you get, you must give. It seems appropriate to me now that I would have some kind of religious explanation for my loss on the heels of such a "religious" experience. I fantasize a fish-angel swooping down and stealing my net. It just couldn't have floated away. And I'd make the same offering again for the thrill of that moment.

M'Lissa reminded me later of a different religious interpretation of the experience. I spent hours locating gear for the trip, arranging the details, giving them instruction, playing guide, and probably made a total of twenty casts of my own that morning on White River. She explained it as karma. I gave of myself to them, and in return I caught the biggest trout of my life and actually got a picture of it. While that doesn't quite explain the loss of the net, I like it.

In the end, I suppose Catholicism, Hinduism, Buddhism, Islam, Judaism, and probably most of other religious "isms" have a notion of reciprocity at the core of their credo. You get back what you give out. In "Fishism," a sect of Paganism into which you could say I've been baptized, you can focus on what you did to lose the net, or you can focus on what you did to catch the fish. I choose the latter. Then again, why do I need an explanation at all? There was a river, a big fish, the right imitation, a good net, Hanalei and me. We all came together in a moment of time to create an unbelievable experience…and a little mystery.

A Rainbow trout I caught on the Whanganui River, New Zealand, 2009

The Fly Fisher's Dilemma

Once when I was talking with a woman at a party, the conversation went in an interesting direction when I said, "I like fly fishing." She asked if I killed them. "No," I answered, "I'm strictly catch and release," quietly taking pleasure in my purity. To which she responded, "Oh, so you only traumatize them?" Having read David James Duncan's response to a similar critique of this sport in his book, *God Laughs and Plays,* I was prepared to debate the issue if pressed by pointing out that I'm actually saving the lives of dozens of flies. But her playful, snarky little jab pricked my conscience. "Yeah," I admitted, "I only traumatize them." Then I quickly added, "But I also make them smarter next time." Herein lies my dilemma. I love the sport of fly fishing, but I hate thinking that on average one in ten of every fish caught and released dies shortly after being freed, or so I'm told.

I love how fly fishing forces me to fully engage with nature and stay fully present on the river. It necessitates gingerly wading over slick boulders while leaning forcefully into rushing current to avoid losing my balance and maybe my life. It requires watching for rising fish and concentrating on the surface to see what they might be taking. It demands attending to my knots, my drag, and my tippet, especially when fishing for wild Redsides on a big river like the Deschutes. I relish guessing where a fish is holding, what it's feeding on, and then testing and confirming my theory. Nature pulls me in and awakens the ancient predator in my cells and DNA. I know I traumatize them and that some even die afterward, but the primitive hunter in me can't stop fly fishing.

Rivers that traverse the floors of deep canyons take me to prehistoric times. The glacially slow changes recorded in walls of stone from millennia of water rushing over them transport me to another epoch. This happens to me in the Deschutes Canyon. Also cutting its way through a million years of granite is White River, which joins the Deschutes River. This river has formed its own impressive little canyon within the larger Deschutes Gorge.

One time in early spring I fished the lower section of this river below the falls, which already looked a little discolored from the heat on the glacier that feeds it. There are not a lot of fish in this river, but there are some big ones. The biggest one I ever caught came out of private water above the falls, so naturally I wondered whether the lower section held equally large fish. I suited up, stuck a bottle of water and granola bars in my vest, and started my trek down the steep path near the falls.

Hiking in this narrow canyon reminded me I was in my late fifties. My muscles felt weaker, and when I slipped it seemed harder to recover my balance. I got dehydrated more quickly, and tired more easily as I walked on landslides of shale boulders that provided perfect homes for every kind of cold-blooded snake imaginable, including rattlesnakes. As I pushed beyond the stretch where the bait casters usually stop, I thought, "Enjoy this day because you are not going to be able to fish this canyon for many more years."

I started fishing about three quarters of a mile downstream from the falls. It didn't take long to figure out that an indicator was mandatory. The big fish lie deep in the boulder-strewn runs, which makes it tricky to get a decent cast to where they are. A tangle of Ponderosa pine branches and high bushes eliminate your back cast, leaving a roll cast as the only option—not my forte. Big trout in this river don't get that way by accident. They are smart enough to lie on the side of the river where most fishers aren't traversing and behind boulders fishers can't reach. They're also lurking on the bottom between the rocks. That way they don't have to work to hold position, which means you are going to lose flies trying to get to them.

Here I had to act on one of the bigger revelations in my nymphing education—get the fly down to where the fish are. The smaller the fly, the more important it is to obey this rule because fish may have pea-size brains, but they can quickly subtract the amount of energy required to eat the fly from the amount of energy it will provide once consumed. A negative score means the fish doesn't move.

I stumbled over rockslides, crawled in narrow passages through huge old bushes, and nearly fell in a couple of times. I managed to land a couple of beautiful smaller trout, although they might have been steelhead smolts, since I was below the falls and above the Deschutes confluence. I would roll cast, watch the indicator for a few feet, then lose it as it submerged, leaving me fishing by feel. Some fishing purists eschew indicators; I'm not one of them. The only way I can fish without an indicator is if I keep the line taut and gently pull it through the current using a high sticking approach. That way if something hits it, I feel it immediately. I prefer a dead drift with the current, and for this you need an indicator because your line won't always stay perfectly taut if you let the current have its way with your bug.

After an hour I climbed on top of a huge boulder on the river's edge at the bottom of a run. A bedroom-sized boulder sat in the middle of the stream just out from me. Below me a chute led to a slight waterfall. In other words, if I wanted to land a fish in this stretch I might have to go with it through the chute. From this platform I had a bird's-eye view of a run. I could see that the current swirled around a smaller boulder at the top of the run and then merged and dropped into a somewhat narrow, slightly darker-colored trench running down the middle. Bordered on both sides by shallower water, the trench went deep enough to provide protection and slower moving water. It had to hold fish.

My boulder perch allowed an over-the-left shoulder, straight downstream back-cast, which somehow I managed to accomplish. My fly landed just to the right of the upstream boulder. The current ran faster than I thought, but three small lead shots seemed to be enough to get the fly down, and after a few feet pull the yellow Styrofoam indicator a couple of feet below the surface, but still visible. I fixated on it and saw it pause for just an instant. I suspected the line was caught on a submerged rock. As I raised the tip, I realized that this was no rock. A surge of electricity shot through my body as the fish dashed toward me, and I madly stripped the line to keep it taut. Then that fish screamed full-speed straight upstream with my yellow floating line bending in the current trying to catch up. The fish fought like it knew it had size on its side. Then it turned and headed downriver where its size and the current merged to multiply its strength by a factor of ten. Damn!

The Fly Fisher's Dilemma

I stripped line as fast as I could and then felt the slack burn through my fingers as the fish raced past me and turned toward mid-stream. It stopped dead behind the huge bedroom boulder. Line on the reel, back under control, I couldn't move the fish. What was I thinking bringing a 5-weight on this river? At least I had 3X tippet. Then I realized that's only on the top fly. Oops. I only had 4X tippet on the dropper fly, which I had no doubt it took. Of course at the moment I realized my error, the fish headed for the chute downstream. I held the rod high and gingerly scooted on my butt off the stone perch. If I was going to land this fish with 4X tippet, I was going to have to wade the edge of the chute where the water ran a little slower, but also where it undercut the bank below a big old pine tree and a low hanging branch. I managed to hold the arched rod in one hand with tip in the water, lift the branch and duck under it with minimal water over the top of my waders. This fish still wasn't stopping! I held on tightly as we both toured the next fifty yards of current going downstream.

I told myself he was tiring and saw a stretch of slower back water along my bank just a bit downstream. This was where I had to make my stand. I slowly tilted the rod to shore and this monster rolled on its side briefly and went with me. With my rod bent in a semi-circle, I reeled in slowly as the fish reluctantly came upstream. I got it right to the bank. I reached out to land him. Too far! Damn! My indicator made it impossible to pull the fish close enough to scoop it with my undersized landing net.

This was a big fish! A vibrant red streak painted on its side flashed in the sunlight as it rolled again momentarily. I had to move my indicator down the line so I could reel him closer. I reached up, quickly grabbed the line with my thumb and index finger and tried to push the indicator down the line with my other fingers. Of course at exactly at that moment, a combination of a little head jerk, fragile 4X tippet, and a dead spot in the line where I was holding it was enough to end our torrid relationship. That beautiful fish turned slowly, caught the current, and disappeared in an instant.

So not only did I fight it to near exhaustion with an undersized rod and too light of a tippet, but in the end I left the fly in its mouth and accidentally released it before it was fully revived. I stood there feeling like an idiot for making a rookie mistake when my irresponsibility hit me. This incredible work of natural, living art might be too exhausted to regain its balance in the current. It might very well be at risk for its life.

I fished for another few hours with stronger tippet, but the memory of that fish haunted me for the rest of the day and all the way driving home. At least twenty-four inches long, that trout could easily have been ten years old, maybe older. And that day I not only didn't land it, I might have killed it. What a depressing thought. I hate thinking that something has to die for my moment of pleasure, especially something old, wild and gorgeous. I can live with incidental kill on hatchery fish, which are given a chance at life for purposes of sport, but incidental kill on wild fish feels near unbearable, especially big wild fish.

A few days later, I found myself on the internet googling "proper catch and release guidelines." I wanted to reassure myself that the fish had lived. I found myself at the Ontario Ministry of Natural Resources, Fish and Wildlife Branch, Fishing Section website. It had an article titled, "Catch and release angling: a review with guidelines for proper fish handling," by S.J. Casselman. The author had reviewed 118 catch and release studies involving 120,000 fish. How do scientists do a catch and release study, let alone 118 of them involving over a 100,000 fish? I eagerly dug into the report.

Across all studies the average mortality was 16 percent. I thought it was 10 percent. The studies involved different species, but still, that brought the kill rate to one in six. A number of factors raised the odds of releasing a fish to fight another day. Barbless hooks caught 22 percent less fish, but had a significantly lower mortality rate. Barbs tear tissue and subject fish to pathogens in the water that can infect and kill them weeks later. Fish hooked in the throat had the greatest mortality rate. Cutting the line in those instances reduced mortality from 58 percent to 36 percent, and 60 to 74 percent of fish released with hooks in place managed to discard the hooks by the end of the studies.

Pathogens could also kill a fish if it lost too much protective mucus. Of the four types of landing net mesh types compared (rubber, knotless nylon, fine knotted nylon and coarse knotted nylon), the knotted mesh types resulted in greater injury and mortality than rubber or knotless nylon. While my net did not touch that huge fish, it would have qualified as the least acceptable. Another strike against me. I had tried to save a little money with a cheap coarse knotted nylon net after losing my expensive soft knotless nylon laminated one to another giant fish on this same river above the falls a year earlier.

It came as no surprise to read that if the fish bled, mortality went up dramatically from 16 percent with no bleeding to 40 percent with profuse bleeding. In Cutthroats it went even higher to 53 percent, but if they didn't bleed, mortality was only 6.5 percent. If they didn't bleed and the water temperature was 8 degrees Celsius (46 degrees Fahrenheit) mortality was zero, although it climbed to 8.6 percent if the water temperatures were 16 degrees Celsius (60 degrees Fahrenheit). This boded well for my fish, as this river runs glacier cold even at twenty miles down from the mountain.

I wondered about landing time. One study found that fish that were chased for ten minutes (which is about what I remember in my case) or less had an 88 percent survival rate. However, survival dropped to 62 percent for fish subsequently subjected to the air for as little as 30 seconds, and an astoundingly low 28 percent for fish exposed to air for 60 seconds. For fish that did survive, those exposed to air for 30 seconds took two hours for their heart rates to return to normal. For those exposed for 180 seconds, it took four hours to return to normal, assuming they lived to recover.

These important findings suggest that we should leave the fish submerged in the net as we're extracting the fly. Since my fish never left the water or touched a net, I took some solace in these last couple of findings. I also felt relieved that the odds seemed high that it would throw or dissolve the hook within a short time. I surmise that pathogens prove less lethal in cold river water than warm lake water, so any torn flesh would likely heal quickly without infection.

In the end, I settled on an emotionally functional resolution to my dissonance and concluded that my fish probably lived. Still, every time I hit the river, I wrestle with the reality of incidental kill. I don't know how to resolve it except to strictly abide by the research findings. I now use fine knotless mesh nylon or rubber nets only, and fish with smaller hook sizes and of course pinched barbs. For a while I even passed on the fabled Deschutes stonefly hatch where size eight and six hooks are common, and potentially more lethal. Now, instead of fishing alone, I try to fish rivers with buddies, so one can handle the net as I land a fish and vice versa.

If we track back the impact of most everything we do—drive, eat, wear clothes, or even buy a book, something gets killed or dies along the value chain. It's tough being conscious of this inevitable consequence of being part of nature. However, we can leave a lot less death and destruction in our wake if we always remain very aware of the price other beings pay for our lifestyle and choose accordingly.

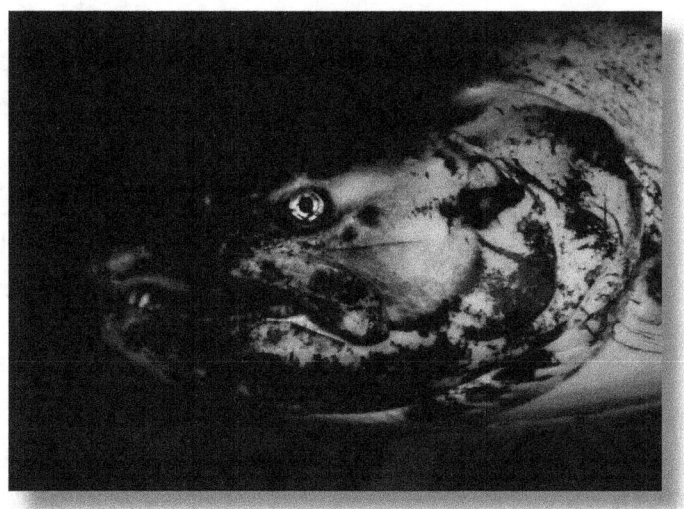

*A spawned-out salmon in the shallows
of the Salmon River, 2010*

Mitch: The Tao of Rivers

The Salmon River, a quintessential steelhead river in Oregon, became a major reason I wanted to move from San Francisco's Pacific Heights neighborhood to a little town near Mount Hood called Rhododendron. With headwaters in the Huckleberry Wilderness of the Mount Hood National Forest, it runs through an old growth Douglas fir, hemlock and Western red cedar mixed conifer forest with occasional alders and vine maples lining its banks. I love the size of this river. It runs fifty feet across and shallow enough to wade in some places and ten feet across in others where it races at full speed through impassable lava chutes.

The fly fishing only section starts at the Salmon River Road bridge and runs six miles up to a falls. A cross between a salmon and trout, steelhead salmon's instincts take them to sea and back again two or three times if they're wild. Their trout instincts make them at home in fresh water and comfortable staying resident for a few months after they're born and just before they spawn. When the runs were healthy, the steelhead used to get stacked up like cord wood below the falls. Their migratory journey ended there. But many of the steelhead that ended up at the falls were hatchery born. Genetically lost, the innate homing device that brought them up the Salmon River was meant for another river from which their eggs originated. Unfortunately, they would never find their true home and fortunately they would rarely reproduce and dilute the wild gene pool native to the Salmon River.

In the fall, as the alder leaves started turning yellow, then orange, red, and brown, the diehard fly fishers on the mountain would get up before light to position themselves near a favorite hole at the first sign of morning. I would not go to the fly fishing only section, but to my favorite spot downriver. I would park near the golf course and with flashlight in hand, head out in the dark across the dew frosted 10th fairway to where the river skirted the rough and trees. Lots of raspberry bushes grew wild there making the rough even rougher. I always had to look for that one familiar small opening in the bushes that created the doorway to the narrow path that wound around and through the sticker bushes to the ten-foot eroded bank overlooking the river.

I'd climb down the bank holding on to a big tree root, slowly wade across the river and head upstream about one hundred yards, staying well back from the bank. Steelhead can feel you coming. They can hear you stepping on rocks, scratching them with your cleats, slipping and splashing as you try to recover your balance. You have to employ stealth and patience or you wake up your quarry, which has been lulled into a false sense of security by eight hours of darkness. Fish think (to the extent they think) that if they can't see you, you can't see them.

My favorite hole started with a riffle that flowed into a run under some bushes along the opposite bank. I usually sat a little downriver and waited for first light so the fish would not see me. I would sit in the cold, sometimes rainy darkness and watch pairs of salmon on their redds. They would be swimming side by side, buck and hen. Sometimes one would show a burst of energy and the splash would break up the repetitive sounds of the riffle or the rain drops on the leaves. I could see the gray blotches on their heads and backs. They had accomplished their mission and were dying. The next day as I crossed the river I would see their carcasses on the river bank downstream.

Autumn on the Salmon River feels utterly bittersweet—such a beautiful scene, yet with the sight and pungent smell of death. With this backdrop, I would step quietly to the river's edge, pull off fly line, make a short distance cast, then a big mend with the line running slightly downstream from the rod, and let my Purple Leech or Skunk Green Butt or Peach Glow Bug swing slowly back to the shallows to entice a steelhead.

It usually takes about ten to fifteen minutes for me to land a steelhead in the Salmon River. Unlike trout, fighting steelhead means using muscle and patience. I've gone home with carpel tunnel syndrome more than once. Steelhead "takes" give you a total rush. Your heart hits 160 in five seconds. But not all takes happen like this. Steelhead may take a glow bug like a trout and you won't even know they're on until you think your line is caught and you give it a tug. Suddenly…BAM! The water explodes with fury. A glow bug works as a salmon egg imitation, which can be deadly for steelhead. Fishing lore says that steelhead on the move will position themselves below a salmon redd knowing that in the flurry of activity to lay the eggs and fertilize them with sperm, some eggs will be shaken from the egg skein. Delicious little morsels floating just below the surface, salmon eggs make a nice little early morning protein hit for a road weary steelhead that's gathering strength before the next push upriver.

You can get other "takes" on a leech or bug imitation. Territorial and aggressive, the steelhead sees a big colorful fly slowly swinging toward its position in the act of trespassing. The fish moves a couple of feet upstream, turns and attacks the fly with the current at its back. You feel this powerful jerk and sustained pull that yanks your bent arm straight. Your rod and line go perfectly taut as the subsurface force of nature makes a run for freedom, maybe breaks water and does a head stand. Inevitably you find yourself being forced downstream in an effort to gain control.

I don't share my favorite holes with many fishers, but I did show one guy who had lived on the mountain for years and intrigued me. I met Mitch Williams, one of the mountain's true environmental warriors, when the locals were fighting to save a section of North Mountain from being sold by Clackamas County to raise money for a golf course it wanted to build outside of Portland. We fought the project for two years, which ended up costing the county two million dollars due to the reduced price of timber by the time the sale went through. He and I drank a few beers together in memoriam after this native forest got clearcut by a greedy asshole I won't name. I like knowing I pissed the asshole off enough for him to call me a communist (not much of a reach with a name like "Marx"). And I still think he should have thanked us. We saved him a couple million dollars from his original bid.

Mitch worked as a fireman in Portland, Oregon. Slightly introverted and a big feeling type, he was divorced and raising his son. A long-time steelheader, Mitch used spinning gear. He took me fishing one evening early in the season and showed me a part of the river I had heard about but never tried. The drill involved putting a little financial offering in a rusty coffee can on the front steps of an old cabin and then walking over to the fence that signaled this was private property, opening the old barbwire gate, and walking down to the water.

We fished for about an hour before Mitch landed a hen. A hatchery fish, most guys would have thumped it and taken it home. I would have. Mitch fought it like a guy who had caught hundreds of steelhead, brought it in to the shallow current, and gently took the hook out of its mouth. "What a pretty fish," he remarked as he held it in the water to revive it. Mitch then barely lifted the steelhead out of the water for a split moment, looked the fish in the eyes and kissed it on the beak. He turned to me with the smile of a river sage and said, "I always kiss the first steelhead I catch in the New Year in honor of my father who taught me how to fish and all creatures and their habitats." We kneeled on the bank and talked while waiting for the fish to revive. When Mitch released it, the fish swam swiftly back to safety. Mitch was no ordinary fisher.

To return the favor, I took Mitch to my favorite stretch of water. He hadn't fished this water before and I was delighted I could show him a place on the mountain he didn't already know about. On this somewhat chilly and misty morning we had this stretch to ourselves. I put him in all the best holes. We worked it hard, leap frogging each other downriver.

As I swung my fly through the last great hole, the sun started to hit the water. Sun on the water usually signals the end of playtime on the river, at least when it comes to steelhead. They get spooked when they think they can be seen. I tried to hit every inch of the last good water before the sun touched it and then started to wade downstream toward Mitch. He was standing about ten feet off the bank, looking down. He hardly moved. As I approached he slowly raised his head, put his index finger to his lips, and signaled for me to stop and be quiet. I froze, still wondering what was going on. He kept looking down into the river a little to his right. Then he bent over and reached down into the water as if he was feeling for something. After a few moments he stood back up, looked at the sky, took a deep breath, shook his head and smiled in a way that said, "I'm a little blown away at the moment." He pointed upstream to a salmon redd. "The salmon that made that redd just slid back to where I was standing and has been leaning up against my boot this whole time. I've been standing here with it for about ten minutes. It let me stroke its body. Then it finally let go."

We both knew that when a salmon falls back from the redd, it no longer has the strength to fight the current and has given in to death. Why it stopped to rest by Mitch's leg I'll never know. The answer involves the physics of water and currents, but I think the Tao of physics that Mitch brings to the equation has more to do with it. He has a connection to nature that few people have. He respects trees, mushrooms, beavers, and fish as members of his community. When they are threatened, he comes to their defense. When they're holding tenuously to the last thread of life, he's grateful to share the moment with them, show respect for their long and difficult journey, and honor their passing.

Plenty of guys would have just kept wading and missed the gift of that moment. I think some would have even freaked out a little and pushed the salmon away, hurrying its descent into death. Mitch knew he was blessed by being allowed to share the last moments of that Coho's life. I think Mother Nature was thanking him for all the years of work to protect that mountain and all its inhabitants. Mitch knows and truly loves his "place" and it knows him. The more I'm out in nature with people like him, who have dedicated their lives to protecting it, the more I'm convinced that Mother Nature lives as a sentient being with intelligence and benevolence beyond our comprehension. She endures the most heartless exploitation and still shows us the face of this earthly "god," if we have eyes to see it, ears to hear it, and hands to touch it. And like she did with Mitch that day, if we make an effort to protect her creations, she finds a way to say "thank you."

With Laura in New Zealand, 2009

The Marriage River

"Marriage is a river. Sometimes it's easy rowing, sometimes it's scary hard, and sometimes you get caught in an eddy going nowhere but round and round." Laura must have thought that casting our latest emotional rapids in these terms would help me keep things in perspective and remain optimistic. For the most part her reframing worked. I was fifty-five years old, we had been together almost twenty years, and I thought we had come to the beginning of the end. Admittedly, I can be fatalistic.

Looking back on it now, twenty years appears to be a watershed moment in many relationships. Or staying with the river metaphor, it's the Class VI rapid—the one you work around instead of carelessly running. At the time I remember thinking, "This is my Rainie Falls moment." Rainie Falls is a Class VI rapid on the Rogue River in Oregon. It's the only impassable rapid from the put-in at

Graves Creek to the take-out three days later at Foster Bar. Those foolish enough to run the falls straight on will almost certainly bite it. Rainie drops about ten feet with giant boulders in all the wrong places. Only the most skillful and daring guides attempt it and only in high water. Of course the occasional alcohol-emboldened idiot will try to run it, sobering up just as the raft starts to crest over the falls. A few unsuspecting novices have also learned the hard way the value of reading the river guidebook in advance.

Those of us who are not guides, drunk, or rookies on the Rogue approach Rainie Falls with respect by pulling over to river right. We then go through the slow, laborious, clumsy, and occasionally dangerous process of roping our rafts and hard boats down a natural "fish ladder" that circumvents the falls. It requires a team effort. One guy stays in each craft while the rest line up at about fifty-foot intervals along the winding and rushing water near critical points where an assist is needed. Each person tries to straighten out the raft as it comes downstream. You can't row in the narrow passage so the one person in the raft uses a single oar in a Huck Finn-like maneuver to push off the boulders along the bank. Let there be no doubt that getting through the fish ladder is an unartful necessity, not an elegant performance of oarsmanship.

In our twenty years together, with the help of Jungian psychologists as "guides," Laura and I had navigated a couple of Class IV and V emotional rapids, but this one felt more perilous. I subconsciously suspected we would come to this point one day, being two strong-minded, independent, first-borns. Over the years, I had watched some of my friends' marriages approach the falls and I hoped we could avoid it with things like good communication, engaging in common interests, not overworking, taking vacations, and having regular sex. But no, we hit rough water just like so many others in my circle of friends.

While most of my friends married in their early thirties, I dragged my feet until my late thirties. Most of them had kids. We chose not to have them. While kids can be relational glue, they can also become a major distraction for a couple. When the last child hit high school, a good number of couples I know started to hear the low roar of a waterfall downstream. In previous years, sex had become less frequent, intimate, and enjoyable. Some of them began sleeping in separate rooms to get a good night's rest. Romantic escapes were spaced further and further apart. Jobs started taking more time. Movies, concerts, and nights out dancing together required too much energy. They talked too much about the kids. They watched too much TV. They bought too big of a house and had too much stuff to fill it up, and then had to work harder and longer to pay for it all. Each couple had been married just shy of twenty years when they hit the falls.

With some of the men I know, twenty years of marriage coincided with the approach of age fifty. Around this age they stopped evaluating what they had accomplished from birth and shifted to evaluating what they wanted to accomplish before death. This existential milestone made it harder for them to continue to suppress their feelings, interests, hopes or passions.

Some of my friends tried to compensate for the holes in their marriage by having affairs. Others tried to close their eyes and hearts and resign themselves to living with less. They ran Rainie Falls blinded by denial and capsized, losing damn near everything including their boat. Others seemed to think they could run the falls without a guide. "If we need counseling it's already over," one of my friends told me. Like others, he and his wife had deferred the maintenance on their marriage so long that it *was* beyond repair. The suppressed anger and resentment created dry rot that spread so completely through their marital craft that it shattered upon hitting the rocks. Casting their mate as the problem didn't help. This position surely lands a couple upside down in turbulent waters. The truth is one's mate is 50 percent of the problem…at most.

For us, stepping into the river of marriage meant a journey of personal growth, individually and together. Before this class VI rapid, we pulled into a relational eddy we'd circled in before. It was time to delve more deeply into the dynamics of this eddy. We worked with a couple's counselor to guide us. It took us a year of working hard to get out of the eddy and around the falls. At times it felt like we were wedged sideways in the fish ladder with little hope of getting unstuck. Dealing with emotions felt like navigating with one oar and constantly banging against boulders that spin your ass around and knock you completely off balance. It was chaotic, humbling, raw, and embarrassingly clumsy.

In the process of working through this period, we acquired new relational skills and knowledge about ourselves and each other. I remember saying to the therapist, "I'm smart. I should be able to figure this out." He responded, "This has nothing to do with being smart. What you think you see or hear is not necessarily what's really happening." The surface water does not always reflect the powerful undercurrents at play. We had to be willing to delve into the dark undercurrents between and within us. Catharses that came in tearful moments of truth and understanding re-oriented our relational bow downstream.

Every married couple travels down an uncharted river. Their individual and collective backgrounds, personalities, life experiences, fears and aspirations create their own river and rapids they must eventually negotiate. No perfect river guidebook exists because every couple's river is unique. So when they hear a growing roar of emotional rapids in the distance, they are wise to pull

The Marriage River

ashore and seek assistance from a wise guide who has helped others transverse their rapids.

In these disorienting times, some couples pull over to the bank, split up the gear, and hike out alone to try and understand themselves and how the river of their relationship got to this troubled point. But in my experience, the journey to truly seeing the truth about yourself comes when you circle in the eddy, bang up against the boulders together, and rope yourselves down the fish ladder. Navigating troubled waters together helps us truly discover who we are and what we're capable of being, individually and together.

I came to appreciate Laura's metaphor of a river as a way to frame the relationship. If you keep this in mind, you'll see marriage as more than a contract, a partnership, or vow never to be broken. It will remind you that marriage is a process. Expect difficult passages and challenging rapids. Expect slack water that forces you to find ways to keep things interesting and make progress. Don't be surprised by surprises; even familiar rapids change over time. Stay awake, and never take the river for granted because even a simple Class II can take you under. Keep practicing the skills you'll need together to handle very rough water. Know each other's emotional strengths and weaknesses so you can support each other in moments of vulnerability. Recognize that what you see on the surface is not necessarily what you have to fear or understand in order to survive. And give up this relationship killer: the need to be right.

When I view marriage as a river, it never ends until it ends at "death do us part." There the river meets the ocean and we paddle into the sunset. Until then I stay committed to running this river with Laura, getting better and better at reading and handling the rapids together. Since our last emotional rapid, we have made our way through a few Class II and III waters that at one time could have gained current. In the boat together, we continue to learn about ourselves and our own unique bond and connection.

I'm not sure how this river trip ends, but I do know I want to reach my highest emotional potential in a deep and lasting love. At the time of this writing, Laura and I have been married thirty years. We give thanks for our hard work in the past. Seeing our journey as a river has helped me shed my fatalism. On to the next rapid.

Kirk, circa 2000, describing the fish that got away.

Tell Me a Fishing Story

One afternoon Kirk sent me an email saying he couldn't get his mind off an upcoming trip to Oregon to fish the stonefly hatch on the Deschutes. He was having no luck at trying to do anything that would justify billing a client so he flippantly wrote me, "Tell me a fishing story." He probably assumed he'd get a couple of sentences or reminder of a fish one of us caught on a previous trip, but I too felt distracted with anticipation about the same trip. I decided to take the bait and see what I could crank out. This is what I sent him an hour later:

It was a cool, sunny, fall Friday morning when I decided to blow off work. I packed my gear and jumped into my Toyota pickup, and I headed for the Deschutes. An hour later I checked in at the Deschutes Canyon Fly Shop and learned that a few fish were coming to the surface, but not many. I picked up a couple of size 18 Pale Morning Dun (PMD) imitations, pale green. I cruised up the frontage road on the east side of the Deschutes to one of my favorite spots outside of Maupin. After taking some time to get my waders on, I sat in the cab while the sun warmed me up and ate a great eggplant, basil, tomato, feta, and balsamic vinegar sandwich. I drank a cool Arizona Ice Tea and treated myself to Honey Dijon Kettle Chips. I listened to Bruce Springsteen's *Tunnel of Love* CD and thought about Laura and our first dance at our wedding reception. We danced to the title song, "Tunnel of Love," and I wondered whether it was the most appropriate choice for the occasion. But one thing I did know—we nailed that first dance.

At 1 P.M. I finished lunch, put on my boots, rigged up my rod, and tied on a little PMD. I locked the pickup and walked slowly to the river side of the road, crouching as I approached the ledge of a steep shale embankment. Carefully I scanned the riverbank, my eyes moving methodically upstream when I saw probably the biggest dark wild Redsides I had ever seen on this river. They were sipping PMDs off the surface. Four of them lurked just ten feet off shore. My heart started racing. I watched them for a while and took note of a large boulder near them so I would know where to land my cast from downriver.

I walked downstream and started slowly descending over the shale rocks on a not-so-stable path that traversed the embankment. It took me about five minutes to get down to the stream below. I slowly got in the water and waded up about thirty feet below the marker rock. I waited, seeing that they were still coming up at regular intervals. I let some line out while keeping my eyes on the surfacing fish. Occasionally one would porpoise and I'd see its huge head. One of them probably measured twenty inches.

I started to cast the line, but the wind made it difficult. Finally, I landed the fly on the water about two feet below them. After retrieving the fly and seeing them still coming up, I made a couple of false casts to gauge my distance and released the line on the third cast. This time the fly landed inches to the right of the outer most fish. The fly hit a little seam, turned, and a head came out of the water and sipped it. I lifted the rod, the hook set, and the fish leaped out of the water, splashed down with a crashing thud, and sprinted full speed right at me. I stripped line as fast as I could but the fish kept going. With my line barely taut, the fish raced past me heading downstream. As he hit the current, the line burned between my fingers as the stripped loose coils flew off the water's surface and onto the reel, which began to scream as it approached the maximum RPMs. While nearly impossible, I tried to adjust the drag down slightly to control the rate at which I let the line out. I had only 5X tippet on a tiny fly, and I knew I'd lose the fish if I clamped down too hard and too fast on the drag.

With the line now unreeling at warp speed, I could see the yellow backing starting to show up below the last few coils of dry line on the reel. The fish leaped again downstream. The last twenty feet of line shook off water as it hit the air. The sunlight flashed off the spray. Suddenly the line on my reel turned yellow as the dry line ended and went into the backing. I tightened the drag slightly, thinking either I turn him now or he'll spool me. The fish didn't slow at all, and the line was still racing off the reel. He approached a riffle where the river started to pick up speed. I thought if I can't stop him before he hits the fast water, he's gone. I tightened the drag slightly again. My heart still pounding, I tried to hold my rod perfectly still and tilted toward shore with no quick jerks. With it almost totally bent over, I was regretting using my new pricey, perfect casting but under-powered Loomis GLX 5-weight.

Just then the fish hit the top of the riffle, leaped a third time, and cleared the water by about a foot and a half. My entire dry line nearly went airborne. In midair he shook his head side to side and stayed airborne for probably ten feet. He hit the water and then POP! The line went dead.

It felt like a minute passed from take to escape, but it all happened in about fifteen seconds. I stood there stunned. I dropped the rod tip onto the water while my heart rate dropped back under a hundred. "Wow, what a fish!" Total awe and respect swept over me. I never had a chance to catch that beast. In no hurry, I reeled in the line thinking that between the 5-weight rod and 5X tippet I had blown this encounter. Then I saw the fly still on the end of the line, leaving a little wake as I retrieved it. I looked at the PMD and realized in amazement that the end of the hook was broken off. Was it a flaw in the manufacturing? Was there a spot of rust on the shank? This was a new fly, right? Or did I pull one of my older ones? Incredible! I turned and looked upstream to see if its friends were sipping flies again. Nothing. It was quiet and stayed that way while I sat there and waited.

After about twenty minutes and a couple of worthless casts, I climbed back up the bank, took out a cold Black Butte Porter and rested on the tailgate of the pick-up. I thought, what an amazing sport! It makes for such great story telling!

Kirk said he liked the story; it even gave him goose bumps! He hadn't expected to get more than a paragraph. Eventually I told him the story was actually true, although a seamless coalescence of three different encounters. They all happened on the Deschutes though.

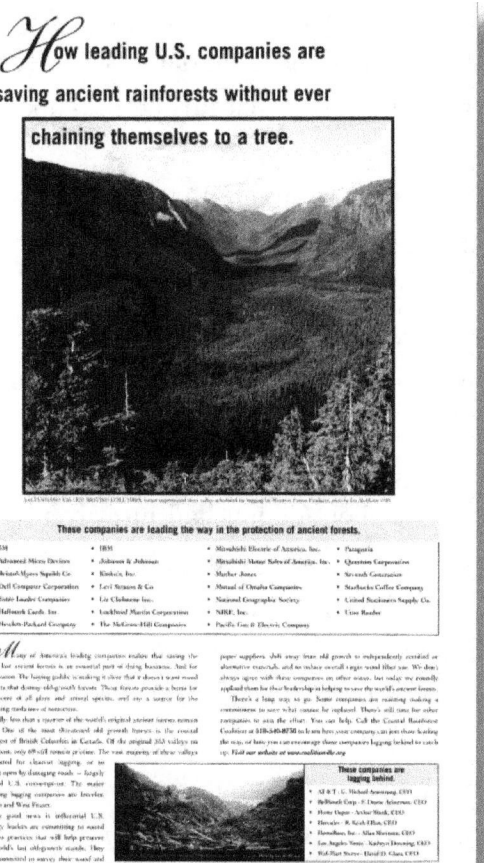

This full-page ad ran in The New York Times on December 8, 1998.

Fishing for Lunkers

To me, when I fish I am essentially engaged in an act of persuasion. I throw out a fly that convinces my quarry to bite. Then I do whatever necessary to get it into the net. Fishing can also be seen as a metaphor for how we change the behavior of others to satisfy our needs or achieve our goals. We fish for compliments, explanations, even dates. Two decades ago I took a three-month "fishing" trip that turned into one of the most consequential of my life.

In the fall of 1998, Laura and I were living on Clear Creek in a little town called Rhododendron at the base of Mount Hood. We owned a beautiful old two-story cabin allegedly built by the Jantzen Sportswear family's grandparents in the 1930s (or so the real estate agent told us and we took the fly). Although I would hardly wet a line during the fall steelhead run, that season I caught the most and biggest "fish" of my life.

W. Alton Jones Foundation had just given the Coastal Rainforest Coalition (CRC) two hundred thousand dollars for a public campaign to stop logging in the last sixty-eight pristine valleys of the Great Bear Rainforest. The CRC included Greenpeace International, the Rainforest Action Network (RAN) and Natural Resources Defense Council (NRDC). The funding came with the condition that a senior-level director manage the coalition. NRDC hired brilliant lawyers, scientists, and policy wonks, and didn't always appreciate Greenpeace's free-wheeling modus operandi. Greenpeace hired smart, hard core, adrenaline-driven activists. So did RAN, but that didn't mean that RAN and Greenpeace were always simpatico either. My job was to keep these brilliant, headstrong activists on the same page.

Leading an international boycott campaign against Mitsubishi, the largest corporation in the world, turned out to be nothing compared to trying to manage a coalition of three of the most diverse, media-hungry and results-oriented environmental groups in the world. Before I came on board, CRC directors, Chris Hatch of RAN, Tzeporah Berman of Greenpeace International, Marc Evans of Greenpeace US, and Liz Barratt-Brown of NRDC had sent out letters to 1,700 of the largest corporations in America. It requested the companies find out from their suppliers where their wood and paper products came from. If they came from the Great Bear Rainforest of British Columbia (BC), the letter asked them to discontinue those purchases. The letters made brief front page news in BC. The mailing not only tweaked Canadian nationalistic and provincial pride, but more than that, it threatened their timber industry's largest market—the United States.

CRC hired Mike Brune, a savvy young former Greenpeace canvas director from San Francisco (who would go on to become the Executive Director of RAN, then the Executive Director of the Sierra Club), to follow up with the companies. For eight months, he had had a modicum of success. A few companies actually checked with their suppliers and sent letters back to the CRC either acknowledging they had BC pulp in their product lines or denying it. Few if any of the companies cancelled contracts with the named timber companies.

We needed to light a fire under these companies' asses. A few weeks after I started as their director, I got an idea to try to "fish for and catch" these corporations. I proposed we send a letter to fifty companies that raised the stakes. The letter started out nicely enough saying, "We need to demonstrate to logging companies in British Columbia that major corporations like yours no longer wish to purchase unstainable old growth wood products." Then it made it clear that in ninety days we would be running a full-page ad in *The New York Times* saying that we "asked industry leaders in the US to help us save the last intact ancient rainforest in North America." The letter concluded by saying that in the ad, their company would either appear in Column A (those that agreed to take the steps we asked) or Column B (those that did not). Either they would be recognized for taking a stand against logging in BC and old growth forests in general, or they would be embarrassed for refusing to do so.

The letters went out in mid-August and included an official commitment letter we had drafted for them. We gave companies sixty days to send back the official commitment letter on their company stationery and signed by a senior officer. Sixty days didn't give an environmental manager much time to move a major procurement policy change through the bureaucracy, but logging companies like Interfor, Western Forest Products and West Fraser were moving heavy equipment into some of the last pristine valleys on the BC coast. We had to move quickly to send a clear message to the timber industry and the BC government to stop logging these valleys or risk losing millions of dollars in contracts with their corporate customers in America. We had never tried this kind of tactic before, and the big question was whether we could land enough of these corporate fish to pose a credible threat.

In the early going, the fishing went relatively easy. We hadn't realized how much "old growth forests" had become like "mom and apple pie," even to corporate executives. It seemed that none of the companies wanted to be in Column B, the bad column. They especially didn't want to be in Column B if their competition was in Column A, but getting into Column A wasn't going to be easy because they would have to change their procurement policy for paper and wood products to consider their sustainability.

Some companies were all but in the creel. RAN had already obtained commitments from Mitsubishi Motors and Mitsubishi Electric as part of their deal to end the boycott against them for Mitsubishi Corporation's rapacious logging activities around the world. Mike Brune had obtained commitments from Nike, 3M, and Pacific Gas & Electric through persistent and skillful persuasion. We just needed to get the commitments on paper. Other companies like Mother Jones, Seventh Generation, Patagonia and Utne Reader were inclined to commit, but even they had to get agreement with their magazine and catalogue publishers.

When my rookie partner on this fishing expedition, Judy Goldblatt, and I started casting for the major corporate players, the fishing got a lot tougher. Some companies refused to answer our calls. We couldn't even get them to look at the fly. The Home Depot, Home Base, and some of the large lumber retailers couldn't be bothered. We didn't expect them to give us a second look and had sent the letters to them as more of a formality. We wanted them in Column B because we planned to go after them with a high visibility public campaign.

We referred to other companies as the "dark stars" (a la Star Wars fame). Dupont, Dow Chemical, and a couple of others fit into this category. We thought they probably wouldn't make the commitment, and we really didn't want to give them good public relations anyway. If we did, the rest of the environmental movement would have crucified us. Still, we worked them hard. Sure enough, we negotiated commitments from three out of four dark stars. For reasons I never really understood, they didn't want to be in the ad. We didn't want them in it either. We all agreed that if they made the commitment in writing so we could share it with their suppliers, we'd leave them off the ad. We got what we wanted and avoided an internecine conflict with other environmental campaigns that would have objected to giving the dark stars positive environmental public relations.

Other companies chased the fly but they never really took it. After going back and forth for a couple of weeks, Wal-Mart finally told me in a polite Arkansas accent that "we're doing some recyclin' and explorin' some energy savin' techniques in our new stores. We think that's enough for now. Been nice talkin' to ya'll." Into Column

B they went. I didn't like the company anyway. The *Los Angeles Times* was buying pulp from BC's rainforests, and its owners arrogantly refused to meet our demands. They fell into Column B in the ad, but later a team of their reporters would do a great feature story on the logging in the Great Bear Rainforest. I like to think our ad motivated the staff to compensate for their management's poor judgement. AT&T, which was doing some pretty progressive work to go paperless, insisted on debating the life cycle feasibility of our demands. My college debating experience helped me go a few rounds with their in-house PhD, but it seemed he cared more about winning the debate on how to approach it than saving a rainforest. Unfortunately for AT&T, his truculence landed the company in Column B. The debate was over. He lost.

The hardest work involved getting the giant fish like Bristol Myers Squibb to take the fly, keeping them on the hook while they fought to escape, and landing them. I flew to New York to meet with an executive vice president, and when we sat down to talk the first thing he said was, "We don't like the tactics groups like Greenpeace and Rainforest Action Network use. Instead of hanging off smoke stacks they should be more professional in their approach." I quickly realized this encounter called for an entirely different fly. I pulled out my metaphorical Purple Egg Sucking Leech for the occasion (the one I often used for steelhead). "Well, that's one of the reasons I asked them to let me talk with you first," I said. "Your company has a good environmental reputation and I told them we can accomplish a lot more through professional discussions than banner hangings off your New York high rise."

We were getting results, but slower than I hoped. Big fish are not easily spooked, lured or fooled. After repeated calls, Starbucks, IBM, Dell Computers, and Advanced Micro Devices finally sent commitment letters. After Bristol Myers Squibb came on board,

Fishing for Lunkers

we used them to get Johnson & Johnson to come through. Lockheed Martin, of all companies, made the commitment. I said to holdouts, "Look even Lockheed Martin has made a commitment to end old growth paper purchases! We're talking mother and apple pie here! Surely you can make the same commitment!" I used this tactic with Este Lauder, and we used their commitment to get Liz Claiborne into Column A as well.

We were getting down to the wire. Underground Media had completed the ad design. On December 8th *The New York Times* would print a special environmental insert in its Sunday Edition and it would include our full-page ad. We had some huge corporate names, but I was after one holdout: Hewlett-Packard (HP). When I talked with its senior environmental manager I remarked, "I can't believe that Hewlett-Packard, one of the most enlightened high tech companies, is going to let IBM be in Column A while it's in Column B. I just can't believe it!"

At thirty minutes to the drop dead final design sign-off, I made my last cast. "Look, I've got ten minutes before I have to call my graphics people to finalize the ad. Are you going to let HP be known as a company that wouldn't act to save the last ancient rainforest in North America? What will your employees think? What will your customers think?" The fish moved to the fly. "I'll call you back in ten minutes," he said resolutely. Twenty minutes later, he called back. "I just talked to Boise. We're in. I'll fax you the letter right now." We got 'em! The ad went to final copy.

We netted thirty companies in seventy-five days. We contacted the PR firm, Communication Works, run by Michael Shellenberger, and they thought we had a great story they could pitch. A few days later, Shellenberger called saying that CBS News would run the story if we gave them an exclusive the night before the ad ran. We agreed and instantly I started to shake all over. Realizing the impact a CBS

News story would have, Tzeporah Berman, who had led the fight for Greenpeace in the Clayoquot Sound battle and knew the BC government well, warned us to prepare our companies for a backlash. Tzeporah was presciently seeing serious thunder and lightning on the horizon. The companies needed fact sheets and preparatory calls because once this news story hit the media, the BC government, timber companies, and public were going to attack them.

The night CBS News ran the story, my heart was pounding. Dan Rather introduced the segment, then John Blackstone started it by saying something like, "Tomorrow in a full-page ad in *The New York Times*, several of America's leading companies will announce an end to the purchase of old growth forest products." As he began his report, the logos of all the companies began to appear on the television screen. This was a big deal! The story included a clip from Chris Hatch of RAN, who repeated one of his favorite lines, "In this day and age, logging old growth trees for wood is as barbaric as killing elephants for their ivory." In his final line, Blackstone compared our strategy to save old growth trees to the one that saved dolphins from tuna fishers. Wide-eyed, Laura turned to me. "You did it!" "We did it," was all I could say, shaking my head. Then I broke down crying, and she hugged me.

I knew we were using these companies to save a forest. They were doing the right thing, but they had no idea they were about to take a public relations hit in BC. It scared me to think they might try to collectively undercut our effort. What if they backed down? This had become a high stakes game for the reputations of the companies, government, and CRC's NGOs. These were not just big fish. These were great white corporate sharks, and a school of them. What made us think we could keep control of this drama we put in motion?

The next day, *The Vancouver Sun* ran a banner headline about the ad. Canadian television news stations gave us the equivalent of a million more dollars in coverage. Our BC allies were thrilled by the flood of interview requests yet fearful of the potential backlash against them. The BC Minister of Forests was calling the companies in the ad, sending them timber industry and provincial propaganda by overnight mail, and scheduling visits to "educate" them on BC's "world class sustainable practices." BC companies were threatening IBM and HP with contract cancellations. Timber unions were threatening boycotts of Hallmark's greeting cards. Timber towns were threatening Starbucks outlets with boycotts.

Nearly all of the companies stood their ground. Este Lauder and Nike were the most courageous with their public comments. Three companies appeared to backtrack. Hallmark made some weasel response to the BC media. Starbucks put up a letter to customers in its BC stores that appeared to soften its position, but didn't really. IBM was the only one that really backed down when its BC office pressured corporate headquarters to soften its stand. IBM?

The BC press posted exaggerated headlines, claiming that companies were backing down in the face of pressure from the province. It wasn't true. The BC press was displaying its provincial bias trying to show that the province could stand up to big US corporations. Unfortunately for them, we released the letters the companies had sent to us with their commitments in writing on their stationery signed by senior executives. It worked. *The Vancouver Sun* had to run a story acknowledging that when it reviewed the letters and queried the companies, in fact they had all agreed to end purchases of old growth wood products, especially from BC's rainforest, and had not backed down. This quickly got the backlash under control.

When I first proposed the idea of the ad, CRC directors never imagined it would become this big of a news story. Honestly, I didn't either. When the news cycle subsided, there was no doubt in the BC government or timber industry's minds that CRC was a force. We could move the biggest corporations in America. We embarrassed the BC government for its horrible logging regulations. In the process, we sent a strong market signal to every timber company in North America that they would risk their reputations if they logged old growth forests, and the practice must end.

The CRC's battles to save the Great Bear Rainforest Campaign would go on for another two years before The Home Depot, Lowes and three of the largest home builders in the US would agree to our demands. When the campaign ended, BC's Premier and the CEOs of the three timber companies stood on a stage with us and First Nations chiefs in front of the entire BC and Canada national press and announced the protection of over 2.5 million acres of the Great Bear Rainforest. Due to what became known as the Joint Solutions Process between First Nations, environmentalists, and BC timber companies, within two years nearly five million more acres would be protected. And thanks to CRC and its successor, ForestEthics (which would later become Stand.earth), within ten years a total of nearly eight million acres—over 80 percent of the forested areas of the Great Bear Rainforest—was permanently protected.

During the three months of the full-page ad strategy, I can't tell you how many times I walked out of our little A-frame office on Clear Creek and stood on the bank praying to the giant Douglas fir and hemlock elders across the stream. If a higher collective consciousness operated in nature, I wanted it to help us pull off this feat. Whether it helped or not I'll never know, but I do know that during that fall, I definitely caught the biggest fish of my life, and it helped save the largest remaining intact temperate rainforest in North America.

Captain Willard (Martin Sheen), emerging from the river to carry out his orders to execute Colonel Kurtz.
Permission of American Zoetrope Productions

Apocalypse Now: A River into the Heart of Darkness

There are a score of great river movies like *African Queen, A River Runs Through It, Sometimes a Great Notion, Deliverance, Mystic River,* and *Emerald Forest*. But to me, Francis Ford Coppola's *Apocalypse Now* ranks as the greatest river movie ever.

When *Apocalypse Now* hit the theaters, I saw the Vietnam War as an archetype of hell. I feared being there worse than eternal damnation. The stories that returning veterans told reinforced my fears. The ordeal of war haunted them and had wounded them inside and out. Hatred for this war shaped me and my generation.

Coppola constructed his story around the rivers in Joseph Conrad's *Heart of Darkness* and Dante's *Inferno*. The entire movie depicts an allegorical descent into the darkest primordial regions of the human heart as it tries to make sense of and survive the horror of war. It is an acid trip from sanity to insanity and back again to a kind of "sanity" that can only come from participating in the sanctioned but deeply disturbing immorality of war. At the beginning of the movie, General Corman (Gervase Duan "G.D." Spradlin) briefs Captain Willard (Martin Sheen) on his mission to terminate US Army Colonel Kurtz (Marlon Brando), who leads a rogue battalion of natives. Higher Command fears Kurtz has lost his mind. Corman sets the stage for this complex morality play when he says, "In this war, things get confused out there—power, ideals, the old morality, and practical military necessity ... because there's a conflict in every human heart between the rational and the irrational, between good and evil. And good does not always triumph."

The making of the film itself became a descent into hell. Coppola faced funding challenges throughout, a typhoon destroyed the sets, and Brando arrived massively overweight and completely unprepared. Martin Sheen had a heart attack and lost his father during the filming. He also did not act the infamous scene in which he drunkenly shatters the mirror and lacerates his hand with an ill-directed karate move. It really happened. Actors became chronically sick. Dennis Hopper was allegedly taking every drug known to man at the time, which prepared him well for the role of a crazed photojournalist. Shooting fell far behind schedule and went well over budget. As scripts were finished at the last minute and improvised during the shoot, the story began to write itself. The meta-story of *Apocalypse Now* became a documentary as Coppola's wife recounted in her film, *Hearts of Darkness: A Film Maker's Apocalypse*, and documents the unfolding descent of the project and cast into the darkness.

As the story unfolds, the muddy river that we vicariously navigate with the increasingly unhinged crew on a plywood military craft acts as both security and vulnerability. Motoring through a military encampment under fire at night, the river and boat protect the crew from the hallucinogenic nightmare of a Vietcong attack on an American outpost by a river. Being on a boat passing through the chaos seems to mask their presence while affording a frightening front row seat to the drama. Yet when the crew steps off the boat the next day, they're attacked by a wild tiger. As they motor farther upriver, they become vulnerable to natives' primitive arrows when they unexpectedly start shooting out of both sides of the forests, affording no escape. We watch the river shrinking as they go deeper and deeper into the jungle and come closer and closer to the evil encamped at its source.

When they arrive at their destination, madness surrounds Willard and two remaining crew members. They land to a world of Haides, the Greek God of the Dead. Decapitated bodies and severed heads are strewn about. Corpses hang from trees. American soldiers and native warriors have painted themselves for war. Insanity rules. Crazy and genius become indistinguishable. The deeper one sinks into the hallucination, the more macabre it becomes.

Captain Kurtz has embraced the irrational as a necessity of war. He talks of the "shear brilliance" of a Vietcong enemy that can cut off a child's arm because American GIs had vaccinated it. No questions, no mercy, no remorse. "It is judgment that defeats us," he tells Willard. The Vietcong's complete separation from judgment of their actions, feeling for their victims and sense of morality gives them power over villagers who are caught between warring tribes with fealty to neither. To Kurtz, defeating this kind of enemy requires one to become like them—and worse. More primitive than its enemy, Kurtz's Montagnard tribal army wins battles that more traditional forces cannot. But Kurtz has crossed over; his absolute disconnection from feeling and morality has made him an insane sociopath.

Kurtz's loss of all feeling grows like a gangrenous wound, infecting, weakening, and ultimately poisoning his psyche. "Sometimes I go too far," he tells Willard, knowing that he is mortally wounded by what he has lost as a result of what he has done. He knows he cannot go home again, and that Willard arrived as his executioner, but also his escape from the darkness that envelops his being. Kurtz wants Willard to know what he has learned about the evil of this war in hopes he will carry this message back to the war's proponents.

When Willard rises from the river in primitive face paint, steam rising as if from hell, and as the community prepares the ceremonial and allegorical slaughter of a water buffalo, he becomes the ritualistic high priest. Bearing a machete, he enters the unguarded cave to fulfill his appointed role. As the drums pound and tribesmen cleave the water buffalo mercilessly to death, Willard performs the same ritualistic slaughter of Colonel Kurtz, who utters his final words: "The horror. The horror." These words reflect what he has done to others, what Willard has done to him, and what war does to everyone who dares look too closely upon its horrific countenance. The loss of feeling required to engage in the otherwise immoral acts necessary to win makes a warrior in the extreme, who becomes either a psychopath who feels nothing or a suicidal depressive who cannot expunge these feelings from his life. Both are sides of the same coin and comprise the currency of war. Both leave a wound that if survived, never truly heals.

Other war movies capture the grim realities of war. *Platoon* portrays a cinematic nightmare; *Saving Private Ryan* a shock to the senses; *Gallipoli* a depressing quagmire of wasted lives. But only *Apocalypse Now* takes us deep into the river of psychic insanity of war.

*One of the many Rainbow trout I caught
on the Whanganui River, the North Island, New Zealand, 2009*

Fishing New Zealand

The Whanganui

After five years as the executive director of Corporate Ethics International, I qualified for the first half of my sabbatical. Laura and I headed first to Australia for three weeks, then to New Zealand, where I fished with a guide three times. On my first guided trip I experienced the North Island's Whanganui River.

My guide gave me a choice. We could fish a river that would have lots of action including big Rainbows or Browns, but not the quintessential huge New Zealand Brown trout, or we could fish a river where we would see very few fish, get maybe one or two casts before they spook, and even if we do everything perfectly they may not take the fly. However, the Browns would be huge. Of course I'm supposed to take the second option. Go for the trophy, the once-in-a-lifetime New Zealand Brown. But being an action junkie and feeling a little rusty on my casting skills, I chose door number one. Door number two would be my choice when we got to the South Island and I had worked the kinks out of my technique.

Unbeknownst to me when I booked him over the internet, my guide had competed internationally as a member of the New Zealand national fly fishing team. He told me that the Czech Republic and France consistently win the international competitions—go figure. He not only took me to the Whanganui, one of the four rivers competitors fished when New Zealand hosted the world championships, but to the section of the river he scored the most points of any fisher on one of the days of competition. Lucky me—my guy really knew this river and how to catch fish on it.

Since we saw no dry fly action on the surface, we nymphed all day with a dropper. The day started with a few nice fifteen-inch Rainbows and Browns. Then I hit my first real fish. After five tough minutes of fighting it, I landed a 3.5-pound Rainbow. I know this because my guide had one of those slick landing nets where the handle turns into a scale when you dangle the fish in the net. Picture time!

By the end of the day, I had landed two more that size and several a bit smaller. I had two others that I nearly landed and I swear were larger but the fly came unbuttoned just as they approached the net. Americans and British fishing enthusiasts transplanted Rainbows and Browns in New Zealand years ago, and they have adapted well to become great fighting fish. Although we fished for only five hours total, in that time I landed sixteen or more fish.

Fishing in New Zealand, having a high quality guide I learned a lot from, fishing in a beautiful wooded setting and catching a lot of big fish all made this day one of my Top Twenty fly fishing days ever.

The Ahuriri River

Our Salvidore Dali camper van

When Laura and I rented a van on the South Island, we had no idea we would have to choose from a collection of vans that looked like throwbacks from the sixties. We chose the one with a Dali-like nude angel. It got people's attention when we rolled into little New Zealand towns.

Definitely wilder than the North Island, on the South Island you see big country. Called "Middle Earth," glacier formed mountains, valleys, and huge, deep lakes make up the central part of the island. Peter Jackson shot and produced *The Lord of the Rings* movie trilogy here. Some of the lakes and rivers have the most gorgeous and mesmerizing jewel-like turquoise blue waters from the glacial silt.

In addition to being known for its hunting, skiing, kayaking, bungee jumping and canyoning, the South Island is renowned for its fly fishing. I splurged for two guided trips on this island. First I fished out of Twizel on the Ahuriri River, one of the premier fly fishing rivers in New Zealand.

We checked into a humble motel on the day newly elected President Obama gave his inaugural speech. It brought to mind what an older bed and breakfast host had told us when we stayed in Napier. She talked about how thrilled New Zealanders felt about seeing America restore its standing in the world with his election after destroying it during President George W. Bush's tenure. She gave us a friendly warning saying "nothing better happen to this president or else America will never recover in the eyes of the world." Having lived through the history-altering assassinations of the sixties, I shared her fears.

The next morning my guide called me and said the weather was terrible, the fishing was likely going to be the same, and I could cancel if I wanted. Ah, what the hell? I went for it. He asked for my preferences in rivers, and I said, "I'd prefer one where we didn't see a lot of other fishers." He chuckled and said, "Where we're going, you won't see any all day." He was right. He had rights to one of the privately owned "stations"—a huge tract of farming and grazing lands for sheep divided by the Ahuriri.

Rainbow trout on the Ahuriri River

After catching only one decent fish, he proposed we stop nymphing for big Rainbows and hike upriver to polaroid for Browns. We walked a long way upriver. Unlike blue ribbon trout streams in the US, which are measured in part by the number of fish per mile, like a lot of rivers on the South Island fishing on the Ahuriri was all about seeing a few big fish clustered a good walking distance from each other.

As we headed upstream my guide said, "I'm going to give you only one piece of advice. When you see the fish start to take your fly slowly say to yourself, 'God Save the Queen.' Then lift your rod tip." Knowing that I had a mental hair trigger when it came to setting the hook, I followed behind him, repeatedly imagining a Brown taking my fly on the surface and saying that phrase to myself.

We walked almost a mile before spotting a big Brown all by itself in a long run. I walked back downstream and very quietly waded into the river. Meanwhile my guide crept along the river bank until he was dead even with the fish. Both of us in place, I threw what I thought was a long cast, but it landed just below my quarry. Fortunately, I didn't spook it. I pulled off a little more line and double hauled a cast above it, but short of its feeding lane. Fortunately again, it didn't see the fly or care to chase it. I thought my guide might be starting to doubt his American client's skills. Under pressure, the third cast elicited a "Perfect!" from my guide. Whew! My image restored.

As the fly drifted ever so slowly into the target zone, my guide gave me a vigorous thumbs up, as if to say, "He's coming up." Then this huge head slowly broke the surface, and I mean slowly. His eye looked right at me. His mouth opened slowly, and just as its mouth appeared to close on the fly, I lifted the rod tip, and my fly came fluttering out of his mouth. The fish completed its slow motion roll and showed me exactly what I had missed—a huge fish. I shook my head in disbelief and heard these words from my guide floating downstream on the wind: "God-Save-the-Queen." It gave this citizen of the rebellious child of Mother England new appreciation of her majesty and the importance of showing her a little respect.

The Hunter River

A glacier fed tributary of Lake Hawea, the Hunter River flows through a beautiful, wide valley covered in high grass, brush and occasional clusters of trees. Well-known for its large Rainbows and Browns, this cold river would be my last day of fly fishing in New Zealand.

It surprised me when my guide showed up with an inboard power boat. I thought I made it clear that I wanted to fish a river,

Life as a River

not the lake. I quickly learned why when he said, "Got a fleece? We have a long chilly ride to the other end of the lake where the Hunter River comes in."

Rainbow trout on the Hunter River

Fortunately, I did have a fleece. Forty-five minutes later with a cold wind burn on my cheeks, we beached the boat, rigged up a rod and headed upriver. I found myself saying my new fishing mantra, "God Save the Queen," over and over. As we hiked upstream, I couldn't take my eyes off this crystal clear aqua blue river. It also struck me how few fish we saw; we saw nothing for probably three quarters of a mile, which in the US on a tributary river above a huge lake like Lake Hawea would never happen. I theorized that these fish get big because they eat their young and the monstrous cicada flies that populate the grasslands surrounding the river. Traditional bug life exists; the guide books suggest early in the season to use pheasant tails, hares' ears and coppers, halfbacks, and prince nymphs. However, you'd never know it from the lack of plant life in the river itself. Confirming my theory, the guide books also suggest that early in the season you can fish with spinners—the classic imitation for minnows.

Finally we came to a bend in the river. Like on the Ahuriri, I tried to polaroid fish, but wind and clouds made it tough. We spotted eight to ten large Rainbows gathered at safe distances from each other, covering about thirty feet of the deepest part of the run. "These fish are spooky," my guide said in a hushed voice, as if they could hear him. "Best to get down on your knees so they don't see you." This was going to be interesting. A modest breeze blew down the valley. Tall grass lapped at my chest. The thought of attempting a forty-foot cast with a large rubber cicada combined with the memory of taking three casts before finally misplaying a monster Brown on the Ahuriri flashed through my mind.

We started with the closest fish at the bottom of the run. I pulled out line, made a false cast to get some length, loaded my stiff 6-weight rod, and released a decent shot that landed even with the fish. It moved away toward the overhanging bank. I still had seven more opportunities. We knee-walked forward a body length and I pulled out another few feet of line. Determined not to embarrass myself with another guide, I gave a couple of false casts then double hauled the cicada close to the feeding lane. "Let that go," said my guide. It drifted right by my target, seemingly unnoticed.

"He didn't spook. Throw it again just a little further into the feeding lane." This time, with clenched jaw and murderous eyes fixed on where I wanted the fly to land, I hit the mark. "That's it!" he whispered excitedly. That *was* it! The trout moved slightly to its left, rose quickly, and took the cicada. I barely got the words "God save..." out of my mouth when that fish, clearly hooked, went ballistic. It ran ten feet upstream, went fully airborne, splashed down spooking every fish in the hole, turned and ran downstream. "Reel, reel, reel!" yelled the guide. "It's headed for that submerged tree!" I jumped to my feet and stripped line like a wild man.

With me running upstream and the fish running downstream together we forced the line onto the reel. Then, line racing off the reel, I tightened the drag a couple of notches while my guide ran to streamside just above the fallen tree. At the last moment I lowered the rod and turned it toward my bank. That was just enough to turn the fish. Seeing the guide in landing position, the fish made a couple more quick runs upstream and to the middle, but as it approached the tree one more time, a deft netting maneuver ended the drama.

After taking a picture, we had lunch to rest the hole. I pulled two more out of there before we moved on and they were just as big and fierce fighters. I marvel at how much raw power is genetically compacted into such small bodies. So ended my adventure Down Under. Next time, though, I'm going for door number two. That missed Brown still surfaces and disappears untouched in my memory.

*Barnes Butte Lake, Prineville, Oregon,
photo by Fay Ranches, 2018*

Unforgettable Moments in My Mental Creel

In my many years of fly fishing, I have had lots of memorable moments I keep in my mental creel. The combination of surprise, novelty, heart-pounding excitement with a dash of earthy aesthetics have made them unforgettable. Here are just a few.

Face to Face

I had never fished with a float tube before. I didn't have anything against it. I just didn't spend much time fishing lakes. I enjoyed fly fishing as primarily a river sport. To me, lake fishing meant trolling with flashers and spinners and other metallic devices to imitate a minnow. Occasionally it meant sitting on the end of a dock and dropping a worm and white corn hoping to entice cruising fish. River fishing entailed finding fish; lake fishing involved them finding you. The latter required patience—not a trait I possessed. Also, the fact that my grandpa fished lakes may have influenced my perception that it was an old man's sport. I've slowly revised this notion as I've aged and acquired a little more wobble in my wade.

One spring my friend Eric Chasanoff invited me to a man-made lake in the Sierras. A year earlier, I turned Eric on to fly fishing. Originally I think he saw it as an opportunity to do the father-son thing with his son Benny. That first trip he spent so much time untangling Benny's line and retying on leaders that he rarely fished himself. Eric didn't get the essence of the sport himself until early one morning on the banks of the Deschutes. He got up early, practiced cast after cast for over an hour, and started to feel and see the fluid wavelike beauty of the fly rod and line in motion. As I emerged half asleep from our tent, rod in hand, he walked toward me with a Cheshire grin and look of enlightenment. "I finally get it," he said. After that Deschutes trip he invested a small fortune into all kinds of fly fishing equipment. When Eric finds something that intrigues him, he totally immerses himself until he becomes a master.

On the Sierra trip we fished for planted Kamloops trout using float tubes. The fly du jour was a green damsel fly nymph imitation. To catch them you cast your full medium sink line, count to twenty, and then strip in about two inches at a time. After a few pulls, you let the line sink a bit and then repeat the motion. This method could easily get boring if it were not fairly meditative and generally effective.

The early model of float tubes meant being submerged to your waist. Merely inner tubes with canvas covers and seats that you straddled with your waders, in it you sat about six inches below the water line. You kicked around the lake with a weird low-rider perspective. If you hooked a fish, fighting, landing, reviving, and releasing it was anything but graceful.

The first day on the lake I had landed a few trout and was finally starting to get the hang of things when I felt a nice tug. Stacked line raced off the apron of the float tube, but then suddenly it stopped. The fish had turned and was charging straight toward me. I stripped line wildly trying to keep it taut. The fish was streaking from down deep toward the surface. I held my rod high, back pedaled like crazy with my fins trying to eliminate slack in the line. Then ten feet from my float tube this silver torpedo broke the surface, flew three feet high in the air, and came directly at me. I could see its eyes bulging and mouth open as if in total disbelief. I must have looked the same to it.

Fully airborne and on a collision course, the fish and I froze in this face-to-face game of chicken that seemed destined to end badly for both of us. At the last second, the fish arched, dove, and hit the water inches from my tube. My line shot like a spear between my legs. He broke the surface again on the backside of my tube as I labored to lift a flipper-impeded leg to keep from getting tangled. Then he dove again. Well-known for going airborne, this Kamloops trout leaped three or four more times, and I'm fairly sure I landed it, but I can't say for sure. My mental tape recorder remembers nothing after the image of that airborne trout coming straight at me, eye-level in mid-air. Hunters talk about coming face-to-face with their quarry—but a fish?

Slo-Mo in Corral Hole

One perfect early June day, Phil, Jeff, and I were fishing at Barnes Butte Lake near Prineville, Oregon. A good ole' boy known as a huckster by the locals, Roger managed the lake and kept all the profits, but his mother owned it. She inherited it when her husband died. Had Roger owned the lake, he would have undoubtedly lost it long ago to a bank or in a court settlement. After squandering most of his inheritance, Roger got the chance to create a private "fishing club" on this lake. To get in you paid $500, got a piece of paper evidencing this payment that never would stand up in court, and thereafter you and your guests fished for $50 a day. To his credit, Roger never broke this agreement with anyone I know, although you couldn't believe a word he said about the frequency with which he stocked the lake.

I like fishing Barnes Butte Lake. You often see eagles soaring around the top of the black and rust colored granite mountain for which it was named. In the fall, hundreds of Canadian geese camp out there on their way north. If fishers spook them, occasionally they take flight, swoop around to the other end of the lake, close ranks and approach the float tubers. Their pellets hit the water like hail and bomb fishers and their float tubes. I swear the geese do this on purpose and take great pleasure when they make direct hits, which in my case, they have made several.

We have often seen deer come to the shoreline to drink. Osprey, hawks, ravens, cormorants, and red wing black birds also congregate here. One time we saw three river otters frolicking near the corral hole all day. Roger said he would have shot them if he had seen them since they were notorious for herding the fish into that shallow inlet and gorging themselves on Roger's meal ticket. Apparently that's how they exterminated the blue gills, which was a real loss since for years Barnes Butte Lake allegedly held the Boone and Crocket record for the largest blue gill ever caught.

That day, Phil, Jeff and I had been fishing nonstop with great success. I had turned Phil and Jeff onto fishing with chironomids and an indicator near the shore and their slow morning turned into a productive afternoon. As evening approached we took a break. We drank a beer, pulled out Wild Turkey and smoked a controlled substance. We agreed to wait until dusk and haul our float tubes down to the end of what we had dubbed "the corral hole." We drank, smoked and watched the water, tantalized by the telltale circular ripples. About an hour before sunset we took off with our float tubes over our shoulders, holding our fins and fly rods. We crept down to corral hole at the end of the lake where trout were now starting to lazily porpoise. Phil got in first, kicked slowly into position, and tried to create as few boat waves as possible. I followed behind him and Jeff got in last.

You know the story when you're stoned, right? Everything slows down. The setting sun paints the lake's surface in pale orange light. It looks like you're casting onto tinted lamp oil instead of water. You hear the yellow-crested black birds in the cattails talking in a high pitched guttural crescendo that almost sounds childlike. Swallows speedily glide a few feet off the water and come so close that you hear a muffled pop as they catch a bug mid-flight. Fish are coming up all around you, casually taking newly hatched mayfly duns off the surface. You can easily get caught up in the beauty of the whole scene to the point of not wanting to disturb it by catching a fish, but then again that's why you're there…or so you think.

Phil tied on a Parachute Adams and after pulling off some line, made a nice slow-motion cast that set the fly gently on the surface film about twenty feet away. It felt like I was watching a movie in slow motion. The fly floated perfectly about six feet ahead of a trout that was doing a slow cruise as it picked off the real version of what Phil intended to imitate. The fly floated perfectly still. The sun's orange reflection grew darker. So did the gray images of the cumulus clouds overhead. As we watched the fly, a dark trout profile slowly and peacefully came from just below the surface. It approached the fly, opened its mouth to ingest its quarry, and then nosed down to continue its subsurface search. The second it felt the prick of the hook, it exploded with a fury that slapped Phil (and his stoned audience) back into real time. The evening quiet was shattered by Phil's low voice yelling, "Whoa! Did you see that take?"

Because the corral hole has shallow water and a clay-like bottom, fish often leave a cloudy v-trail as they high-tail it for deeper water. This one left a wake that roiled the calmness of everything around it. Easily twenty inches, the shocked fish leaped twice as it ran. Phil held on as the fish streaked into his backing. Stoned no more, he eventually turned the fish and worked it into the net after a few final short runs. He had landed a beautiful Rainbow now bathed in pale pink from the sunset. The natural lighting, the fish, and the expression on Phil's face all came together to what would have been a photographer's dream photo. Instead it remains a memory made more vivid by the mental and cannabis chemicals that processed it.

To this day, whenever we sit around after a day of fishing and reminisce about Barnes Butte Lake, this story always gets told in stoned slo-mo technicolor.

The Monster below the Barn House

For several years Paul Franklin owned a fifth share in what we called the Barn House just below Maupin on the Deschutes near the water pumping station. You could walk out of the house, cross a railroad track and head straight down to the Deschutes where a riffle ran a third of the way across the river and sent water sweeping toward the near shore. Fish hung out below that bank because the bushes protected them from above, the run was deep, and the currents funneled the caddis nymphs into the riffle.

Early in my fly fisher years during one trip there I had purposely rested the riffle for a couple of hours before nightfall, knowing it would make the fishing better later. As dusk approached, I eagerly waded out into the lower section of the riffle. After a hot day turned to a warm night in late June, I knew this picture perfect riffle would house caddis that trout love to ingest around dinner time. I tested the deeper water a bit downstream and decided to stay shallow, which makes exiting in the dark a lot less risky. You don't mess with the Deschutes, especially at night.

I put on a Sparkle Pupa Caddis emerger imitation thinking that if the bugs were hatching, it would be the perfect fly to start with before going with a dry adult version. I had my only fly rod at the time, a Scott 4-weight. I refused to allow myself to buy another one until I put in some time on the river and learned the sport. I also hadn't fished enough to know that I should have been using a heavier weight rod on a river like the Deschutes. At the time, I loved the slow action of my Scott rod and that I could feel every jerk of a trout's head or change in its direction as it fought.

My Sparkle Pupa Caddis worked. I hooked and landed three nice fifteen to sixteen-inch Redsides, the Deschutes native. I employed the classic motion of casting slightly upstream, mending and dead drifting the nymph until the line tightened at the end of the drift, and then slowly raising the tip of the rod and giving it a little flick. Sometimes I'd strip it in about six inches two or three times. It amazes me how many times I catch trout with the fly suspended underwater or moving upstream in what must be by all rules of entomology the least natural presentation imaginable. A couple of my Deschutes fisher friends tell stories of how they were fishing with an Elk Hair Caddis and momentarily let it wake at the end of the drift while they prepared to throw the fly back upstream. At precisely the moment they went to lift the fly off the water their rod suddenly froze mid-cast. For a second they thought they had snagged surface weeds, but when the "weeds" sprinted downstream, they realized they had a steelhead on the line.

A little past dusk the surreal transition to night began. I had worked much of the riffle and stood about thirty feet from the bank. I switched to an Elk Hair Caddis, greased it, and threw it a few feet upstream and back toward shore thinking I'd now cover the same water again with a dry. As the fly drifted into the riffle, it had that perfect dead drift that you know will produce a splash any second. The water had a gray luminescent reflection and looked chaotic as it got kicked up by the rocks and gravel below. The waves made little black shadows that quickly appeared and disappeared as my fly floated over a gauntlet of feeding fish.

Suddenly I realized those little black shadows weren't all created by the waves. Like a Maurits Cornelis Escher painting coming to life, many of them were fish heads coming out of the water. I swear fifty fish or more were feeding directly in front of me. They seemed to be attached to an underwater camshaft that would lift ten of them forward, then another ten, then another, all randomly positioned across the riffle. Mesmerized, I temporarily forgot about my fly.

The whole scene ranks as the weirdest and most fascinating visual experience I've ever had on a river. The scene became even stranger when I regained my focus and lifted the tip of the rod slightly to discover I had a fish on. I steadied myself for the classic trout run, but nothing happened except the line winched out slowly about fifteen feet toward mid-stream. I tried to reel, but nothing doing. Baffled by the oddity of this encounter, I remembered being told that steelhead, especially large ones, will sometimes take your fly and camp on the bottom. In those cases you slap the top side of your rod to send a vibration down the line. What the hell, I tried it and the line slowly gave way another twenty feet downstream. I realized I did not have a trout, and with my 4-weight rod there would be no budging this monster. "Hang on for as long as you can and enjoy this because you're never going to land this fish," I thought.

So I hung on. I slapped the rod and each time I did, the fish moved downstream a bit more. The white backing on my line appeared, and I tilted the rod toward shore thinking it might get my quarry to head toward lesser currents. Nothing. I jerked the rod a few times. More line lost as the fish moved farther downriver. Out of desperation I decided to really pull and see what would happen. The line snapped. A 5X tippet was not designed for these situations. I reeled the line in, noticed the darkness and my growing hunger pains, and decided to wade in.

To this day I don't know what I hooked, but it must have been huge. It could have been an early arrival steelhead. It could have been a salmon. I still can't believe it didn't run. No head jerks. No quick moves. Just a continual repositioning farther and farther downstream until no chance remained to catch the monster in the eerie waters below the Barn House.

A Lake trout caught and released on the Nuyakuk River, 2015

Alaska: Bucket List

The Nuyakuk River

Where the mountains climb taller, the lakes span wider, and the rivers and wildlife are wilder, Alaska ranks as one of the two most brilliant and foresighted land investments the US government ever made (the other being the Louisiana Purchase). Because Alaska has a place on nearly every fly fisher's bucket list, we owe a respectful nod of gratitude to William Seward, the Secretary of State who acquired the crown jewel of North America for $7.2 million in 1867.

 Six months after deciding to part with a small fortune and check Alaska off my bucket list, Kirk, Jeff, Wayne and I rendezvoused in Anchorage. The next day we took a puddle jumper flight to Dillingham in the Southwest corner of the state, shuttled to a small bay, and caught a pontoon plane from the Royal Coachman Lodge. The minute we started taxiing into position for takeoff, I knew this would be like no other fishing trip in my life. And it wasn't, starting with the panoramic views of breathtaking wildlands dotted with virgin lakes, endless rivers and a mosaic of forests.

Jeff, Kirk, Wayne and I had barely landed at the dock in our float plane and dropped our gear off in our cabins before we were landing grayling after grayling in front of the Royal Coachman lodge on the Nuyakuk River. It got even better; one of the guides ferried me farther out into the giant back eddy above the lodge in search of bigger fish. He surveyed the water below and said, "There's a huge Lake trout down there picking off little grayling. Hand me your rod." He positioned it along the inside gunnel and pulled out a bigger rod.

He quickly clipped off the existing fly, tied on a stronger tippet, pulled out a four-inch multi-colored feather with a weighted eye and secured it to the tippet. "All right. Throw that baby out about twenty feet, let it sink, then strip it back in short spurts. Let's see if he'll take it." I followed orders, counted to ten and started stripping as instructed. "Get ready. He sees it!" I tensed. "Set!" On command I lifted hard and the rod immediately bent over the gunnel almost to the water. "You got him! Keep it tight!" The fish seemed confused; it dove, ran, then circled the boat with short bursts of energy. When it temporarily approached the surface I was awestruck. It looked unlike any trout I've ever caught…and it was huuuge.

We battled for about five minutes more before the guide skillfully dipped his massive long-handled net into the river and scooped up this gorgeous brute of a fish. My hands shook from the tension and adrenaline. I thought catching twenty grayling in an hour said, "This is Alaska!" But catching a predatory Lake trout in a river *eating* grayling and now in the net awaiting a photo said,

"This IS Alaska!" Fishing like this explains why guys like me save up and finally spend ten grand for what they hope will be the trip of a lifetime. With all the different river and lake options, plus float planes and motor boats stashed in strategic river locations, it's hard for Alaska *not* to be the trip of a lifetime.

Dollies and an E-ticket ride on the XXX River

In what would be an evening ritual, the ten guests at the lodge sat down at tables in the dining room drinking cocktails and wine while awaiting a dinner that would rival any restaurant in San Francisco. Our hosts presented a menu of fishing options for the next day and depending on our preferences, we would be divided up into pairs and assigned our guide. They told us breakfast started at 6:30 A.M. and we needed to be geared up and ready at the dock by 7:30 A.M. Don't be late. Our plan had Jeff and Wayne heading for big water and a chance at King Salmon. Kirk and I would be dropped off downriver, pick up a shallow bottom motor boat stashed strategically in the bushes, and head up a little river with our guide and his dog for the day.

On no other fishing trip in my life did any day, let alone every day start by loading into a float plane. Made in Canada, the De Havilland DHC-2 Beaver has the reputation of being the riveted aluminum workhorse of the American and Canadian outback. Ours could accommodate six fishers and a pilot. That morning and every morning at about 6:30 A.M. we loaded into the tight cockpit and strapped in while the pilot revved up the motor. Then he taxied upriver a hundred yards, turned to face downriver, revved the motor even higher, pumped a gear-like mechanism on the floor, and rapidly accelerated while sprinting downriver, finally going airborne. I had flown in Beavers several times during the Great Bear Rainforest Campaign, and every time it took off or landed felt like an adventure. When I got to sit in the copilot seat, don headphones and converse with the pilot while getting an insider's view of his flight plans, I felt like Fonzi (from the TV series *Happy Days*) and the height of cool.

The float plane dropped us off, and our guide and his excited canine companion greeted us. Our guide explained that "we may have to navigate over or around a few logs to get upriver. This will be the first time on this river this year." Navigate OVER logs? An unfished river? This had to be good! We did a slow motor from the main river, the Nuyakuk, to the entrance of a much smaller river when we began to pick up speed, then more speed. This may have been the first time up the river this year, but our guide acted as though we had purchased an e-ticket to Disneyland. With his windswept golden retriever barking in the bow, his clients leaning into the sharp turns with childish grins, the guide stood in the stern maneuvering the outboard motor with the casual grace of a master. We had to unload and back out of a couple of shallow dead ends, which reminded us (and him) that rivers change course. Our guide was running on last year's knowledge and this year's intuition, which only added to the sense of adventure.

After about twenty minutes, we rounded a bend at full tilt boogie when the motor suddenly slowed. A logjam had narrowed the passage and one large log lay across the river and just enough below the surface to create a small wave. We pulled over to the bank, and secured the boat with the bow close to the log. We climbed out onto the logjam and the guide studied the obstruction. He cupped his chin, tapped his index finger on his pursed lips as he looked at the river just below and above the log and said, "I think we can get over it. Tighten up your life jackets." Apparently he concluded the water rolled just enough over the log to grease the skids for the boat. At least that was his theory, undercut somewhat by the life jacket instruction. We cinched up our vests and prepared to test his hypothesis.

We got back in the boat, floated a bit back downstream, gunned the motor and bore down on the mostly submerged log. At the exact moment we hit the log, momentum and a skiff of aqueous lubricant carried us up and over it as the guide hurriedly pulled up the outboard motor to let momentum finish job. Without the motor and with the bow turned by the current, the boat did a startling jerk to the right and almost threw us out, but the guide dropped the motor into the water, gunned it, jerked us back to center stream, and we were again headed upriver at full speed.

One or two miles later the outboard motor slowed again. We could see in the distance a sandbar along a deep run shaded by an overhang of trees. As we approached the sandbar, we could see fresh fish heads and partial spines tossed about. Closer still we could see paw prints—very large prints. "Bears were just here. We must have scared them off," the guide said as we beached the boat.

The adult male Dolly Varden Kirk caught on the XXX River

The guide tied on a colorful attractor fly and instructed us to cast to the far bank and drift it through the deeper run. Kirk casted first, and immediately hooked a Dolly Varden trout. While a species of trout, dollies are in the char family, which includes Arctic Char, Brook and Lake trout. They're native to cold water tributaries of the Pacific in North America and Asia.

As Kirk fought it we quickly learned that when hooked they don't dash around like a Rainbow or other species of trout. They do the

Life as a River

The adult female Dolly Varden I caught on the XXX River

strangest escape maneuver of all trout—they spin. Neither of us had ever caught a dollie, so we marveled at their chrome bodies and orange spots, some darker than others. Later in the trip on another river we would both catch bigger dollies on mouse patterns that we stripped quickly across the surface. The big dollies would trail them at top speed forming a moving mound of water on the surface as they pursued what they knew would be a complete dinner. The bigger male dollies had menacing-looking heads, but more beautiful coloring with their dark green modeled backs, orange spots, orange-brown bellies, and white strips down their orange tinted fins.

After a few hours and a lot of landed and released fish, our e-ticket ride continued, this time going downstream even faster now that the guide was reacquainted with the river. When we re-entered the estuary leading to the Nuyakuk River, the guide put on big pink and purple streamer flies, which we cast into the slower runs. Sure enough, Sockeye and Chum salmon were waiting and instinctively couldn't pass up what probably imitated an ocean staple they had been feeding on days earlier. We motored back to where we originally met the guide, and before too long we heard the roar of the De Havilland coming to take us home. What a day!

Fishing the Crimson Plume

After Jeff and Wayne spun their martini embellished tales of catching a good number of salmon, we were all easily convinced by our guides to head together to a coastal river in search of Kings.

Another fabulous meal, more wine, a slow retreat to bed, a few more recalled moments from the day, and sleep overtook us.

Damn, 6 A.M. comes awfully early after a long day on a river. At breakfast our guides shared the unnerving news that while we wanted to catch Kings on a coastal river, storm clouds may hang too low to allow passage. A little while later as we ran just under the low cloud ceiling and rain streaked sideways off the windshield, from the copilot seat I asked the pilot, "How will you know if we can get through to the coast?" He answered, "When we get to the end of this narrow valley there's an opening that goes through the mountains just to the north of us. If it's clear, we'll go through. If it's not, we'll do a quick, sharp bank to the right, go back out the way we came in, and try another route farther south." A couple of minutes later and a wall of clouds to the north, he banked the plane forty-five degrees to execute a tight turn and implement Plan B.

The second try for the coast worked and we were soon flying over Upper Togiak Lake, a long mountain-bordered body of water fed by occasional tributary rivers. At the mouth of one small tributary to the lake, our guides told us to look down. We saw a plume of red. Several hundred Sockeye Salmon amassed for an upriver run. The scene reminded me of stories about rivers in Alaska turning red during the sockeye runs. "You could almost walk on the backs of the fish they were so thick," the story went. For the first time I really saw what this meant.

We landed the plane, rigged up 7 and 8-weights with colorful streamers and waded into the river near the assembled collective. It felt surreal to stand at the mouth of a small river to the side of a dull red plume of several hundred fish waiting for a sign from their home river to head upstream.

We casted with the standard steelhead technique: quarter downstream and a slow swing across the current. In this tight bunching of salmon, you don't want to jerk the line or reel it in too quickly; you'd snag a fish and waste a huge amount of time fighting it. You can feel this weird sensation of the salmon repeatedly bumping your line as they jockey for position seemingly oblivious to this intrusive chord. But there is no doubt when one takes the fly.

The boys gearing up for Sockeye salmon fishing

Unlike steelhead or trout, none of our fish broke the surface. Fighting them meant a fun, muscular tug-of-war. The fish runs off line, momentarily relaxes while you frantically reel it back, then it runs off more line, charges, then hurriedly retreats, racing right then left. As a rule, when you hook a salmon, it's hooked. Afterward you deal with the temporary carpal tunnel syndrome, then start casting again.

After several hours we broke for lunch. While I enjoyed catching a few salmon on a fly that morning, I found the flight and the majestic mountain and lake scenery the most memorable aspects of the experience. It reminded me that fishing can be just as much of an excuse to take in the gestalt of nature, and in this case, Alaska, a magnificent geological treasure.

Since the morning fishing did not quite meet the guides' expectations, they huddled to discuss the afternoon destination. They decided to give us a treat. We broke down the rods, loaded back into the Beaver, idled out into the main stem of the larger river, revved the engines, picked up speed and slowly lifted off for our next adventure.

Metallic Beauties in a Mountain Lake

The plane followed the expansive lake for several miles. Filling the gap between two mountain ranges, it mesmerized us. After about forty-five minutes, the pilot started to descend. In the distance I could see our destination—a flat area and small lake on an elevated plateau. The pilot did a half circle maneuver bordering the lake and brought the Beaver down to a beautiful mountain lake named Ongivinuk. We slowly idled over to a shore where the tributary streams flowed in.

It thrilled me to learn that we were going to fish for Arctic Char in this lake. I had always wanted to fish for beautiful Arctic Char, which can get fairly big. Because our morning didn't turn out quite like what the guides had hoped, they decided to exercise their once-a-week option to fish this lake. It had tight regulations, and as a condition of their lodge license, they could not fish it more than that amount. We scored!

A beautiful Arctic Char I caught on Ongivinuk Lake

Warm, copper metallic in color, Arctic Char have pink spots and orange belly, lips and fins. Much like their cousin, the dollie, their fins have the most perfect white strips. Like Cutthroat, I could study this fish for long meditative periods of time. I know that evolution paints its creatures in the colors most conducive to their survival, but I marvel at their incredible visual artistry.

We took out 5-weight rods and tied on colorful streamers. Kirk and Wayne started casting from the shore on one side of the plane,

Jeff and I on the other. We casted out as far as possible, stripped the line back to shore, and were immediately into nonstop fish. The Arctic Char weren't huge, but consistently measured in the fifteen to eighteen-inch range and put up great fights. Jeff and I slayed them! Kirk and Wayne struggled to get action despite using the same flies and technique. Fortunes reversed later when we waded upstream and Kirk couldn't miss while the action for the rest of us went dead. An hour or so later we lifted off the water for the lodge and a gourmet ending to a memorable day.

This Too Is "Fishing"

Being dependent on float planes to access your fishing destination has one significant drawback—weather. After learning firsthand the day before how tricky it can be to maneuver around low hanging storm clouds in narrow valleys, we were easily convinced by gusting winds and a serious downpour to wait things out in the lodge. Two hours later and no change in the forecast, we decided it was five o'clock somewhere in America and broke out the wine, nuts, cookies and assorted treats, and settled in for a serious game of hearts. After a couple more hours, lunch. With rain pounding on the tin roof, we played a couple more rounds of hearts, then broke out our respective novels, realizing the day was lost for fishing. Kirk decided to take advantage of the fact that we had a live-in masseuse. No surprise, her schedule was wide open. The lessons? Get on your computer and practice your hearts game before you leave home. Bring at least one good book to read, maybe two. Don't be afraid to splurge for a massage or whatever pleasure you can find to save the day because when you're spending ten grand on a trip like this, what's another hundred dollars?

Embracing the Fire Salmon

Believe it or not, I resisted our guide's offer to spend a morning fishing for Chum. In the lower US, they're considered the bottom of the salmon hierarchy. Depending on who you ask, these fish win the award for most colorful of their species. Against a backdrop of sea green, streaks of purple, orange, red, and black adorn their bodies in waves from back to belly. Fishers find them fun to catch but no one I know of eats them. I would much rather fight a smaller, wilier fish, than a big monstrous salmonid that requires more muscle than dexterity.

I ended up relenting though, and all four of us set out in the Beaver for a coastal river. The Kulukak River ranges thirty to forty feet across, often with gravel bars down the middle and deeper runs near the constantly eroding, high grass-covered banks. A scarcity of trees explains why you see frequent spots where the clay bank has caved into the river.

After motoring upriver a few hundred yards, we tied on purple streamers with 0X tippet and with 8-weight rods in hand waded downstream mid-river. Kirk stopped first. I waded down farther to the lower beat. Kirk saw action immediately. Things started slowly for me, but from the moment the first fish took the fly, I felt grateful my buddies had not listened to me. What a fun fish to fight! Using heavy tippet means you can cinch down the drag a bit more. The fish still take out line, but they rarely run into backing. More control means spooking fewer nearby fish up or downstream. You get short intense fights, quick releases, and more return opportunities.

For the next four hours or more we would step and cast, step and cast, and then dead drift near the bank. Near the end of each drift we would sweep the fly toward mid-stream. If the indicator dragged for a split second, which it did a lot that morning, it meant

Life as a River

my forearm was about to get another major workout. About five fish into the morning I needed a break.

I stood in the river and did a 360-degree scan of the scene. Mountains streaked with long, green vertical strips of verdant brush and trees separated by brownish-gray shale boulder slides and granite cliffs encompassed me. The contrast of verdant, smooth vertical fields next to giant, ragged darkish stones seemed like a metaphorical description of Alaska. Its ecological richness nurtures a remarkable diversity of life while its rugged and unforgiving landscape and weather protects it from exploitation. Not completely; I found myself thinking about how nature in Alaska reigns as a fierce earth mother, but she can't defend herself against the destructive force from humans, whose greed and disregard for the consequence of their actions threaten this magnificent ecosystem. Foreign companies lobby hard for the right to carve riverine systems into gold mining operations. Oil companies relentlessly lobby to drill more and more wells, filling pipelines and tankers with the very fossil fuel that poses the greatest threat to Alaska's environment when it's burned. On the front lines of climate change, this state is heating up faster than any place else on earth.

But I am on my bucket list trip and quickly move these sobering thoughts to my subconscious. I may be amongst the last generation that experiences the immense beauty and excitement of this place, but I tell myself, "Don't waste your trip thinking about things you can't change…at least not until you get home."

The morning turned into a slightly warmer early afternoon, and our guide brought us back downriver where we had our only lunch cooked riverside that week. On the menu—a freshly caught sacrificial Chum over charcoals on a small weber grill. I couldn't help myself; I had to keep fishing while it cooked. The take junkie in me needed a fresh adrenaline rush to sustain the morning high.

When it came to the taste of different kinds of salmon, my buddies and I land with Chinooks (also known as Kings) over Coho (often known as Silvers) and Sockeye, in that order. Chinook swim deeper so they have more fat and oil for warmth, which makes their meat sweeter and moister. The debate never includes Chum. Like most people who even know Chum exist as a species, I thought they weren't that flavorful. It turns out that's only half right. As we learned that afternoon on the river, Chum taste delicious if you eat them freshly caught. Fortunately for them, the flavor doesn't last long after they move upstream, and definitely fades before they can be packed, frozen and shipped south to market. The indignity of tasting poorly saves them.

A "Fire" salmon caught on the Kulukak River

About an hour later, as our float plane was leaving the water I thought how this morning ranked in my Top Twenty favorite fishing days, and that Chum deserve a better name. "Chum" means chopped up bait fish that you throw into the water to attract your true quarry. Even the lowly Pink salmon (sometimes called Humpy salmon) have a better name. The desire to rename this fish still haunts me. No name I've thought of seems worthy. "Fire salmon" is as close as I've come because of its mix of hot colors. Here's to the Fire salmon!

Catching Monsters on a Mouse

After our morning fishing for Chum, the plane roared off the river headed toward home. It followed the interconnected waterways that lay between mountains dotted with scattered patches of snow. We would have all paid a couple hundred dollars just for the plane ride to see this spectacular scenery. As we approached a small valley, the pilot began to descend toward a small mountain lake. We hit the water with a discernable bump and spray on both sides of the plane. We motored to the shore, unloaded and awaited instructions.

"This is a very short stretch of water," the guide said referring to the meandering feeder stream coming into the lake, "but it's our best chance of catching large Rainbows on mouse patterns. You have to take turns. Who's first?"

I picked the long straw and led the way with Jeff, Kirk and Wayne wading a short distance behind. The guide instructed us, "Bounce the mouse off the far bank and when it hits the water, retrieve your line in very quick, short strips as fast as you can." It took a couple of tries before I mastered hitting the far bank and landing the mouse with a splash on the water, but I got the hang of it. On the third cast—Wham! A big fish hit the mouse with a ferocious take, then nothing. I reeled it in and that big mouse pattern was gone. "That was probably a Pike," said the guide. "Their teeth are really sharp." So much for my turn.

Wayne's twenty-three-inch Rainbow trout he caught on a mouse pattern

Wayne's turn. He threw the mouse up onto the far bank, pulled it off and began to strip. Bang! A beautiful, fat, twenty-three-inch Rainbow took it. "Damn, that should have been *my* fish," I thought.

Wayne got a picture with the fish and Kirk stepped up for his turn. Probably the best caster among us, he bounced the mouse off the bank the first time, stripped like crazy and Bang! His rod bent in half as he uttered, "Holy Shit!" and tensed for the fight. This time I thought, "That's going to put all the other fish down."

The trophy trout of the trip: Kirk's twenty-five-inch Rainbow caught on a mouse pattern

Kirk landed the trophy trout of the trip: a football-shaped, chrome bright, twenty-five-inch Rainbow. I was happy for him, but admittedly envious.

Jeff stepped up for his turn. He made a couple of casts with no action, then moved a little higher upstream. Another cast, and Bang! He hooked and landed a Pike—large by trout standards but small for a Pike. With Pikes, guides take control of extracting the fly from its mouth to avoid sending a client home with shredded fingers. As the guide was pulling the fly out of the Pike's mouth with his forceps, he handed it to Jeff and returned to working on the fish. "You ain't gonna believe this," he said as he lifted another mouse pattern with his forceps for us to see. He handed it to me. "I believe this is your fly." Incredible! The fish took my fly, got stung by it, and still came back again for the same fly. It's hard to resist a mouse.

I tied on the mouse, moved to the head of the line, and whispered a silent prayer to the trout gods to protect me from Pike. After a couple of false casts, a bounce off the bank, a skittering mouse across the water, a large Rainbow crushed the fly mid-stream. A few minutes later the guide netted my twenty-three-inch Rainbow. We took a picture and headed back to the plane.

That hundred yards of river may have been one of the most fun short stretches of water I've ever fished. Few fishing tactics rival stripping a mouse at full speed across the water and fighting the aggressive takes of large Rainbows (and Pike…and dollies) intent on scoring the ultimate meal offered by an arctic ecosystem.

And Then It's Over

The only problem with checking off a bucket list experience is that it too quickly comes to an end. On the float plane ride back to Dillingham I felt wistful, regretting the end of our week. I scanned the landscape looking for bears and moose, two things I expected to see but didn't. Nothing. A last water landing in that little bay, a ride with a young native woman who provides taxi service in the summer to earn money for college, a greasy lunch at a "restaurant" near the airport, and one last night in Anchorage. All of these felt like little mundane steps back down the stairway to the everyday reality of life, which of course by the world's standard of living, isn't the least bit "everyday." I went home in touch with the fact that a week of my everyday life would be on the bucket list of billions of people on the planet. Perspective.

Yellowstone Park's Slough Creek in the second meadow, 2014

Little Boy Fishing in the Greater Yellowstone

When I was a senior in college, Yellowstone awakened me to the possibilities of catching living works of art on an artificial bug imitation and then releasing them. I didn't return until my mid-sixties. What was I thinking?

Years later when I came back with my buddies for a week-long summer road trip, we started calling our adventure "little boy fishing." Over martinis and dinner, we would open a guide book and decide where we would fish the next day. With the anticipation of a little kid, every day presented a new river, a new challenge, a novelty that made this and other trips like it special.

A boy lurks inside every man. He wants to play, have an adventure, and explore the unknown. For six days in greater Yellowstone, the wide-eyed little boys inside us indulged these yearnings and experienced the overpowering beauty of the granddaddy of all national parks and the rivers that run through it.

The Madison River

On my first trip back, Kirk and I rendezvoused in Bozeman, my nominee for the Fly Fishing Mecca of America. We planned to fish a different river every day for a week and christened the trip "The Odyssey II." We started outside the park on the headwaters of the Madison below Quake Lake. Our guide, Ron Sorensen of Chocolate Lab Expeditions, met us at the launch site. We knew Ron; he had guided us in Argentina and lives in Ennis, Montana, half the year.

We drifted a short distance downriver before beaching the boat. Ron tied on a pink hackled foam body Tan Chubby—a killer fly as it turned out. Kirk and I landed several nice Rainbows and Browns. We drifted another short distance and divided up the water. At one point, like all crazy fly fishers, I decided to test the other side of the river. I slowly waded out into the middle in relatively shallow fast rushing water up to my knees. A sheltered run with some depth ran close to the far bank. Casting would be tricky because while the run ran slower, the water I was standing my ground in threatened to grab the fly line as soon as it hit the surface. My plan consisted of casting the fly, doing a mid-air mend, and just as the fly hit the surface lifting my rod skyward to get the leader and dry line off the fast water. This might give the fly a brief shot at a two-second dead drift with an overly eager fish lying in wait.

I casted, did a half-assed mid-air mend upstream, and raised the rod as high as I could at the exact moment the fly touched down. Two seconds of drift, and BAM! A fierce take, a jerk that said, "Dude, your rod, tippet, and drag are way too light!" This huge

Brown leaped out of the water to try and throw the hook…to no avail. As it sprinted into the downstream current, Ron, who was standing in the middle of the river with a big net at the ready yelled, "Turn him toward me! Stop him before he hits the rapids!" I turned the rod to mid-stream, managed to tighten the drag a couple of clicks, and watched helplessly as that fish stayed to the far side current. I knew chasing him downstream would be suicide. I tightened the drag a little more and then saw Ron lower his net and turn to watch the fish fly by him and around the right bend into the rapids. One final jerk and "Pop!" The line went dead. Gone-baby-gone!

While reeling in a limp line, I mused why I had traveled to New Zealand to catch huge Browns when I could catch them right here. I also told myself to put on 3X tippet and tighten my drag next time. Too bad my best lessons in fly fishing so often come *after* I lose the big one.

The Lamar River

The upper section of the Lamar River generally moves at a good clip through the Lamar Valley, where bison congregate and grizzly bears make surprise appearances in the distance. Quintessential fly fishing water, but we fished the lower Lamar just before it meets the Yellowstone River. Bigger, deeper, and to me more aesthetically interesting, this section cascades out of deep pools into rapids and then other pools. I like this kind of water because it forces fish to quickly decide whether to take my fly or let it pass. I theorize that a pool hosts several fish holding at the top in order to get first shot at a meal. The combination of faster water and competition makes them more aggressive but less cautious. As a result, the advantage goes to the fishers.

This section of the Lamar poses only one major problem, though—the risk of a broken leg. Large boulders make getting to the water an exercise in patience and sure footing. Once there, we had to wade around more and bigger boulders, water sometimes up to our chest. We had to hug the rock banks to access waters untouched by less intrepid fishers. As we waded around these obstacles, uncertainty about depth haunted our every step.

In late July each step through the wild prairie grass and along the river bank scatters hoppers, the fly du jour. Kirk and I surprised several beautiful fifteen to seventeen-inch Cutthroat that afternoon. How do you beat catching big fish on big dry flies in seemingly virgin water?

As we left the river and walked back to the car along the Yellowstone, several massive bison took turns escorting us. In the distance they seemed like big, hairy docile cows intent on one thing: eating. Up close they triggered memories of articles about tourists being gored to death by one of these creatures. We kept our distance.

Slough Creek, Second Meadow

The upper section of Slough Creek runs through a gorgeous high elevation valley. It gets pressure, but not like the Lamar. That's because you have to hike in about a mile to get to the first meadow and over three miles to get to the second one. You have to hike even more if you want to fish its upper reaches. The infamous Slough Creek challenges one's physicality, but Kirk and I thought we were more than capable. Besides, three to five miles in and out means less fishers and more unfished water…and more fun.

We pulled into the parking area near the trailhead and saw very few parked cars. We donned our waders and boots, rigged up our rods, and prepared to set out. We learned later that night that the fishing report said slow going on the upper section. As we walked past one of the few cars around, we saw a beautiful (and I mean pure natural beauty) younger woman getting dressed in the back of her station wagon. Of course we stopped to say hello and asked if she had fished this river before. She had and asked how far up we were going. When we said, "To the second meadow," she took a second look at our outfits and asked, "In waders and boots? You don't want to hike five miles like that!" Out here you don't expect to see a woman fly fisher, let alone be humbled by one. We would have never made it had she not convinced us to wet wade with water-friendly hiking shoes. We jettisoned the sexist stereotype that day.

The hike began with a steady and not so gradual incline that makes one question their decision, especially if this ascent continues. Fortunately it didn't. After three miles I started to feel muscles I forgot to include in my regular workout routine. It took us almost two hours. In the back of my mind a voice kept warning, "This is prime grizzly country…and we're the only guys around." I kept reminding myself that a bear biologist I met during the Great Bear Rainforest Campaign assured me that grizzlies don't generally attack a group of people. I wondered if two constituted a group.

Every few hundred yards one of us let out either a high-pitched whistle (Kirk) or a high pitched "aaaoooo" (me). "Aaaoooo" starts with a drawn out "aaaaaah" and culminates in a loud, sharp, upper register "oooo!" Based on our record of no bear encounters over the last decade, I recommend this or a whistle to avoid a surprise meeting with an unsuspecting mother grizzly bear. And of course we also kept bear spray ready.

Stunningly picturesque, the second meadow spread vastly and easily went a mile or two long. As we walked down a beaten path in the grass mid-meadow, we saw four guys in the process of breaking camp. This river, meadow and island of trees and granite pulled them back every year for a decade. They reported slow action and skittish fish. "Nothing worked, not even hoppers," they lamented. With lowered expectations, Kirk and I divided up the lower half of the meadow and set out. I came to a meandering bend in the river near the edge of the meadow. An old partially submerged snag created a little structure on the other side. As I looked at what seemed like ideal water, a fish rose lazily and took something small on the surface. A few seconds later, it rose again. I decided to use 6X tippet in this slow and clear water with picky fish. I thought terrestrials might be a good play even if hoppers were out. I put on an ant.

A native Cutthroat trout caught on the Slough Creek

With the warning about "skittish fish" in mind, I got on my knees and crept up to the water's edge slightly below the rising fish. Very gently I landed my fly just above him and watched it drift down his feeding lane. On cue, he rose, took the fly, and we were off to the races. When I landed it in the shallows and held it against the black muddy river bottom, the colors of that fish, though subtle, popped. I moved upriver and caught almost the exact same seventeen-inch cookie-cutter version.

An hour and a half dozen fish later, Kirk and I met at another bend up the river. He took one side. I took the other. Even though I had fished my first ant to a shell of its former self, I continued with it and the Cutthroat continued to show it the love! I fished that ant until it damn near turned into a gnat. Then I put on a beetle and still fooled fish. Kirk stayed with hoppers and despite the warning from our predecessors, he too caught fish all day.

We fished until 6 o'clock as to not walk out in the dark. Two hours later we turned the corner into the parking area, hoping to express our gratitude to our fishing muse, and maybe even invite her to dinner. We saw no sign of her, but thanks to her advice I had one of my ten best days on a river. Kirk has said the same about that day. I think this designation came as a result of a beautiful woman fisher, a meandering stream through a grassy meadow, the hyper awareness of being in grizzly country, a long hike and conversation with a good friend, twenty-plus large, wild, Cutthroat, and the anticipation of an ice cold martini at the end the day.

Soda Butte Creek

Kirk and I did a little exploring to see if we could find some less pressured water. We fished the upper section of Soda Butte Creek and hit several different stretches that looked pretty but weren't productive. We decided to test a section of the Yellowstone above where the Lamar comes in, but found it unproductive with ferocious water. No doubt that water held fish, but we needed 6-weights and a commitment to seriously weighted nymphing to get results. We decided to test Trout Lake. While beautiful, we found it equally unproductive. Now nearing dusk, we headed back to our Cooke City hotel for dinner.

As we approached the Soda Butte, Kirk spontaneously asked, "Hey, what do you say we give this section of the river thirty minutes to see if anything's happening?" A martini and dinner sounded awfully good after a frustratingly slow day, but when your buddy has a hankerin' for one last fish, you go with it. The martini will taste all the better for the wait. We walked over to the creek, which couldn't have been more than thirty yards from the road. I'm not even sure we fished the main stem given the small size and slow movement of this stretch. This would no doubt be a quick fish. Besides, this section of the river must get pounded being so close to the rather unspectacular Soda Butte tourist attraction and the road. Any old, and I mean old, fisher could walk to it; no wading required. I decided to hike a little downriver to improve my chances. Kirk gladly took the obvious water.

I caught nothing, but enjoyed the walk, occasional short casts, and peacefulness of this little creek at sunset. At about the thirty-minute mark with no action I walked back upstream. Kirk remained committed. Why? Because as soon as I left, he cast into a mini-riffle that fed into a small pool and a strong, sixteen-inch Cutthroat took his fly and forced him to do some fast walking downstream to land it. I couldn't believe it. In the most unlikely place he caught a fish that seemed way too big for such a small stream. As he told the story, he had the giddiness of a boy shocked at what he had discovered. We walked back in the dark shaking our heads in disbelief. We also wondered whether Yellowstone rivers really get that much pressure if fish such as this one could be caught in such an obvious and accessible location. Another martini and retelling of that catch ended the night.

The Upper Section of the Clarks Fork

How quickly a week-long fishing trip comes to the last couple of days. Feeling slightly sullen that the trip was nearing its end, we decided to head for Cody, Wyoming, and fish the Clarks Fork along the way. The Clarks Fork was named after William Clark, who along with Merriweather Lewis, led the Expedition of Discovery in the early 1800s to map the West, find a suitable route for future pioneers' passage, and establish an American presence before the British and the French. Its headwaters wind through a valley creating an ever-changing serpentine route. Crystal clear water washes its fine gravel river bottom and then darkens to a light shade of green in the deepest spots where the fish congregate.

We got a tip of where to stop, but it would require us to hop a barbed-wire fence and fish on private water. Kirk, being a lawyer and a bit of closet rogue, had no problem with this. While I will do almost anything to fish good water, I found myself hesitating and rehearsing negative encounters with the landowner. Over the years more than once I've said to Kirk, "I'm not sure we should be doing this," to which Kirk has consistently responded with something like, "I know you don't. Let's go." And I always do.

After jumping the fence and going rogue, I headed straight for a logjam where the river bent on its way downstream. Like all logjams, you have to be cautious; one step onto a small log can give way at any moment. You have to take the risk, though, because its structure attracts and protects fish. You also have to think about how you're going to land a fish without taking a swim.

I managed to get a cast upstream with a caddis dry and dropper. There were fish in there alright. A thirteen-inch brookie took the dropper. Fish in this stretch of the river probably don't get any bigger than that. Rivaling Cutthroats for beauty, mature Brook trout have orange bellies with colorful spots. I caught a few more in that hole and then moved upriver to catch up to Kirk. We leapfrogged each other for the next mile and hit deeper runs and riffles. Lots of little brookies kept us entertained.

After a couple of hours, we walked back to the car, hoping to fish farther downriver, which meant bigger water and fish. We stopped at a campground and the docents strongly advised us to keep our bear spray handy. We set out upstream, Kirk periodically whistling and me aaaoooo'ing. In the next two hours we each landed over thirty brookies. They couldn't leave the Elk Hair Caddis dry flies and Hare's Ear droppers alone. After we each touched at least fifty fish that day, none more than thirteen inches, we walked back to the campground where we donated our bear spray to the camp docents for use by other less prepared fishers or hikers. We headed to Cody.

Kirk describes himself as an action junkie. He gets as much pleasure fishing a mountain stream and landing eight to ten-inch fish all day as fishing a big river with less action, even with bigger fish. Me, I like it for a change, but I have to admit that I'm more of a take junkie who loves the rush of a fish jerking my rod into an arc, working the current to shift the odds in its favor, and finally coming to the net, resolving the dramatic tension created by the battle. This trip provided us both with our respective preferences. We left amazed that despite the fact that nearly 3.5 million people visit Yellowstone every year and turn its roads into slow moving caravans, its rivers remain remarkably wild and healthy. Thank you, Ulysses, for saving this natural treasure.

*My 6-weight Scott rod that I broke in a fall
on White River, 2018*

When the River Ends

I wonder how my life will end. Will it be an accident? An incurable disease? Or will I live beyond any quality of life and have to take myself out? If so, would I choose a gun, a drug cocktail, helium, or wade into a river and let go? If genetics predict, barring the unexpected, I should have until my late eighties to choose. Of course by then, wading into a river may require a walker and the world may be out of helium.

Do I want my death to be fast or slow? I definitely choose slow—as in a few months. I want to live every one of my final days knowing that I'm approaching the end. During this time I want to clean up unfinished business, make sure the people I love and respect hear that from me, and pull fragmented memories together to create a collage of what my life meant. From rainbows to the aurora borealis, in the time left I want to feel joy from the things that amaze me. With the melancholy that comes from the simultaneous presence of love and impending loss, I want to feel the poignancy of every kiss, every stroke of my wife Laura's hair, and every burst of laughter. With emotional purity, I want to connect with my lover, family and friends with stripped down honesty to prepare me for the final scene.

Yet I know the final chapter may come as a surprise. I could fall asleep driving and cross a median strip, or get hit by someone who does. A bridge could suddenly collapse and send my car into a river. I could have a massive coronary or lose consciousness from a fatal brain bleed, which is how my dad died. I could also just simply not wake up one morning.

Maybe I'll dodge a bullet, and be a split second on the safe side of tragedy. I could be seated in the passenger's seat when an oncoming car decimates the driver's side. Someone's car horn might trigger my last second brake reaction just in time to make the collision dire but not fatal. Paramedics might arrive and save my ass in what would have been my final minutes. I'll think I used up one of my nine lives and hold on to the myth that I still have a few more.

I can delude myself into thinking I have five of my nine lives left because I've used up four of them. The first: When I was thirty-eight years old and one month before marrying Laura, I was told I had tumors in both testicles and very likely late stage testicular cancer. It forced me to ask myself, "When I'm on my death bed, what will I be proudest of doing?" My then profession of management and trial consultant, making a lot of money, buying a big house and BMW didn't make the list. Instead, it was comprised of the people I loved, those who loved me and the difference I had made in the world. When I asked myself what kind of difference I wanted to make, my heart knew I wanted to help protect forests, rivers, and iconic wildlife like eagles, wolves, mountain lions and bears.

My confrontation with dying awakened my unrealized long-standing life aspiration. So when the urologist called a day before the scheduled surgery to say he had been sent the wrong ultrasound and was canceling the operation, I took it as a gift from my guardian spirits, one I would gladly repay by heading down an entirely different path. I remembered seeing Randy Hayes, the executive director of the newly founded Rainforest Action Network, speak at a conference the year before, and learned that its offices were where I lived in San Francisco. I wrote him a letter volunteering my management consulting skills, and a couple of months later the door opened. It led to a career as an environmental warrior that transformed my life.

The next three of my spent lives involved a river. I tell the story of my second spent life in the chapter "Mike Marx is Dead," when I had a scary encounter on the Rogue River with Jeff and other long-time friends. Spent life number three occurred in Mosier, Oregon. One hot afternoon with close friends I was hiking up a dry lava rock riverbed strewn with boulders. When we decided to head home, it meant climbing up a twenty-foot basalt and dirt embankment. I decided to follow closely behind a woman friend who led the ascent. Being a stupidly chivalrous guy I positioned myself right behind her so if she slipped I could help her. As she neared the top, she screamed my name. I looked up and a monster lava rock ricocheted off the top of my forehead. Stunned, with the sound of my skull cracking, I heard her cry out, "I'm so sorry! You're bleeding! Are you okay?"

That big lava rock exploded onto boulders about fifteen feet below me. Blood dripping down my forehead, brain frozen by the impact, my talons gripped the dirt and stone wall. After a few minutes I surfaced from a dazed mental numbness to see my route upward. With fierce focus I climbed the final length of the cliff.

Only later back at the cabin with a cold wet compress on my swollen forehead did the reconstruction of the story make me realize that if that rock had landed on my head differently it could have easily knocked me out and caused me to fall into the riverbed. Had the rock not bounced off another one just above me, it might have hit my chest, which would have also thrust me to the river floor. The more I thought about it, I realized that if it had happened any differently I could have been paralyzed or killed.

That night, I crawled into my sleeping bag and stared at the star-lit cobalt blue sky. I felt lucky to still be alive. Gratitude flowed like super-heated blood through my veins and brought tears to my eyes. As if a guardian angel was listening, I said "thank you" out loud. In the cool night silence, I imagined hearing the words, "You're welcome. Just don't waste it."

Fifteen years later I experienced my fourth and nearly last spent life. Every spring, Jeff, Kirk, and Wayne or Phil and I would book a long weekend fishing rancher John Justesen's private lakes in Grass Valley, Oregon, and his five-mile private stretch of White River. It's our annual ritual that sweeps the cobwebs from our fly fisher brains and WD-40s the rust in our unused casting arms.

Kirk was the first to cancel because he was diagnosed with a malignant squamous cell carcinoma that would require a major operation on his face and neck followed by six weeks of radiation and chemotherapy. Jesus! Then two weeks before the trip, Jeff was bucked off a horse during a guided horseback ride in the Patagonia region of Chile. He landed flat on his back, fractured his right collar bone, a half dozen ribs, and several vertebrae. He was clearly not going fishing any time soon and suggested I take Jake, his son and my godson, on his first trout fly fishing trip instead.

Jake was excited to learn to fly fish, so we made a plan. Phil joined us, and the first day and half went exactly as planned. We float-tubed a couple of lakes and Jake, already a decent spinner and bait fisherman, quickly got the hang of fly fishing. On the eve of day two, I told Jake and Phil I wanted to go back to White River where I had caught almost all of the biggest wild trout of my life. Phil long ago crossed White River off his list as too damn much work and physically risky. Jake, being a thirty-year-old former competitive athlete and tempted by the allure of big wild trout, signed on.

The next morning Jake and I drove across the high mountain desert, down a windy canyon road, across the Deschutes River near Shears Falls, through the little town of Tygh Valley to Justesen's turn off and road that parallels the private stretch of White River. A couple of miles later we parked, pulled on our waders and broke out the rods with godfather teaching godson about selecting leader weight and tippet, the best flies to use and why, and how to tie them on with a double clench knot. We walked down to a naturally channeled section where I knew from experience at least one big one was surely holding.

With a ceiling of tree branches hovering over the river, we waded cautiously up the edge of the fast moving chute. With little instruction, Jake quickly picked up the art of casting an indicator and two flies sinkers-weighted line without ensnaring it in the overhanging leafy and line grabbing limbs. His second cast hooked a huge trout that leaped out three feet or more, cannon-balled on the surface, threw the hook and escaped. Hyperventilating with anticipation, his fourth cast went a little further across the river, and damn if he didn't hook another big trout that repeated the last acrobatic escape scenario. Since he had stung probably the only two big fish in that hole, I decided it was time to move downstream.

Before the trip, I had a reverie about taking him to this more treacherous spot downstream because it required climbing down a relatively steep and rocky bank with huge downed trees. In my waking dream I asked him what kind of wading boots he had on because if he didn't have felt soles and cleats, it was too dangerous to climb down to the river. My godson was not going to be hurt on my watch!

With Jake following closely behind me, I remember walking deliberately and quickly downriver along a ridge, and approaching the point where we gained elevation and the river dropped into a canyon. I recall thinking about how best to position Jake for the big fish I had caught there before and hoped was still holding there or had been replaced by another. That's the last thing I would remember before waking up in an intensive care unit (ICU).

What happened? Jake knows the most. He remembers me asking him about his boots and directing him down a ridge to a spot on the river, and me walking another thirty feet along the ridge to scout downriver. It was not long before he heard tree limbs snapping and rocks pummeling down the hillside. He called out to me, got no answer, then saw my cap floating downstream. Jake bolted back up to the ridge, rushed downstream, and spotted my contorted body just a foot from the river at the bottom of a long, steep, rocky and muddy embankment. My tilted head and back were slapped up against a huge boulder, and my legs stuck spastically up in the air.

Jake nearly fell climbing down the forty-foot embankment to get to me. When he reached me, it was clear I had somehow taken one hell of a tumble down this embankment. He saw blood coming from my scalp and ears, and asked if I was okay. I opened my dazed eyes and tried to answer, but I couldn't speak. I tried to rise but could barely move.

Panicked, Jake quickly debated leaving me to run for help. Instead he wisely chose to call 911, but his cell phone had no reception bars. He hurriedly searched my jacket and found mine with a single bar. After several dropped calls he finally reached a 911 operator. Within a few minutes, a volunteer medevac team from a small town nearby raced toward the cell phone coordinates. After several over-shots on the road above, they found us. Over the next half an hour, the medevac team hammered big cleats into the ground, secured a pulley apparatus to a tree, stabilized me to a med-sled and winched their casualty up the embankment. Once loaded, the van streaked down the rutted road paralleling the river towards a life flight helicopter that had flown down from the small town of The Dalles. Life flight got me as far as the town of Cascade Locks before heavy winds forced it to land. An ambulance was waiting to complete the relay run to the Legacy Immanuel Level 1 Emergency Trauma Center in Portland, Oregon. From the time I fell to my admittance in the hospital, nearly six hours had elapsed.

Jeff told me that while I was in the ICU unit, several times he asked me, "Do you know what city you're in?" In a weak, raspy voice, each time I gave the same wrong answer, "Mosier." My semi-conscious brain clearly made an unconscious association with my last near-death encounter between a rock and my head, only this time I truly came near death.

"What happened to me?" Laura says I asked her in ICU. I remembered nothing of the accident. "You had a bad fall while fishing on White River, and Jake saved your life," she answered. Laura, Jeff and his wife, and my long-time friend Sue, say that I kept repeating the same line, "I can't believe this happened to me. I never fall." Although it definitely sounds like something I'd say, I don't remember saying this once.

I knew I was in a hospital and couldn't get out of bed. What I didn't know was that I had three minor skull fractures, a concussion, several staples in my scalp, a broken collarbone, a fracture in my scapula and five broken ribs. I had serious bruises the length of my left arm, back and sacrum. Laura says my right hand was so bruised it looked like a black swollen ball.

According to Jeff, while in the ICU, I was hooked up to "a half dozen different machines monitoring my brain and heart." I'm told I had an IV in my arm, a neck brace, and was intubated for a couple of days. I don't remember my time in ICU except the presence of Laura, Jeff, and Sue. In the ICU and subsequently in the trauma unit, I remember several of my good Oregon buddies, friends, godchildren, and my Portland resident niece came to see me, but couldn't tell you when or what we talked about.

After eleven days in the hospital, I went to a skilled nursing unit in Lake Oswego, Oregon, for another nine days. Skilled nursing gave me a front row seat for the boring and painful drama of growing old and being unable to care for oneself. For the first time in my life, I looked in a mirror and saw a gaunt old man leaning weakly on a cane. I came to appreciate the patient and heroic dedication of the nurses, physical and occupational therapists who devote their lives to making this kind of difficult chapter as safe and pleasant as possible. They helped me regain enough weight, strength, and mobility to fly home to San Francisco.

In the second month of my recovery, I began to be able to look through the eyes and emotions of others affected, and grasp frightening details of the accident. I learned that Jake had called Jeff immediately after I left in the medevac van and told him what had happened. Jeff, in shock, immediately called Laura and gave her the cell number of one of the medevac team members who hesitantly reassured her that it didn't appear I was paralyzed. She arrived late that night to see me unconscious, in a neck brace and attached to machines. When Jake arrived at the hospital later that night, Laura told me they held each other for a long time, crying.

Laura and I began to talk more about her experience, which helped me fully realize how my accident had traumatized her, and that she too was in recovery. As Kirk's wife, one of Laura's best friends, put it, Laura "had taken the fall too." She kept having flashbacks of me in the ICU unit and how much she needed rest after long stressful days as my guardian angel in the hospital and skilled nursing. After getting me home safely, she made sure we followed the neurologist's instructions: no falls and get lots of brain rest. Even with these measures, she kept hearing him say my brain may not ever fully recover. In our first month home, she witnessed me looking and acting ten years older. More than anyone, she saw how my brain tired easily and needed sleep, how I forgot agreements we made the night before, struggled with complex decisions I used to ace, often asked her to repeat herself, and quickly lost patience when performing the simplest fine motor task.

Laura was not the only one traumatized. Jeff said he kept having flashbacks as if he was crashing down that canyon slope with me. He could never forget the shock of the call from Jake or the frightening somberness of Justesen saying his river property renter had told him, "We lost a fisherman on White today." Jeff would always remember having to make one of the calls every close friend dreads and then being in the Emergency Trauma Center when my ambulance arrived with a team of doctors waiting, hoping he would not be making another call or having to share in person horrible news most feared by a mate.

Until about four months into my recovery I couldn't evoke the feelings of potentially losing my life. It felt difficult to grasp that my life could have ended. The emotional numbness began to give way and I finally started to sense how lucky I was to be alive. With deep gratitude and Laura's help, I returned to Portland to thank Jeff, Sue and my friends for being there for me and reassure them that I was coming back.

While at Jeff's place, he took me into his garage and pointed to a large clear plastic bag with everything the Emergency Trauma Center team cut off me. We poured out every item, all hurriedly and jaggedly scissored: waders, long underwear, fishing vest, rain jacket, sweatshirt, shirt, t-shirt, even underwear and socks. My eyes kept locking on the dried blood stains. I laid out the cut-up items on the grass, set the destroyed remnant butt section of my 6-weight Scott fly rod and Gunnison reel on top, and took a picture of what was now a graphic metaphor for what had happened to me.

The items the ER cut off me

Then Laura and I headed to Livingston, Montana, for six weeks, just as we had planned pre-accident. It was the best thing for my recovery at that point. Loving the Big Sky's beauty, we began to feel more like "us" again, and romance reappeared in our marriage. Under the watchful eyes of a guide and Laura, with a wading staff I ventured back onto gorgeous little DePuy Spring Creek, quietly ecstatic to be alive and fishing at all. A few days later, because I couldn't drive or fish safely alone, Laura packed a book and folding chair and brought me to a spot on the Yellowstone River where she kept an eye on me from afar. Later on new fly fisher friends kept me under close surveillance and helped me wade some smaller rivers. By early fall, my mobility, endurance, agility, confidence, mental acumen, and self-reliance had seen a remarkable recovery. I still had a slight wobble, needed to meditate and nap, and occasionally searched for words and names I used to know, but in a conversation few suspected I wasn't a hundred percent back.

This accident has changed my relationship to rivers and fishing, probably forever. I now mentally calculate the risks of climbing down steep embankments, wading fast currents in water over my knees, and having to chase a strong fighter downriver. I used to be on the river early and the first to new water. My modus operandi was cast-cast-cast rather than watch-watch-cast. I often waded blindly, fixated on my next casting spot. I would routinely delay and then rush lunch, fish until dark and often afterwards, then go to bed late and exhausted. These days I don't privately count my fish, unconsciously add an inch or more to my captives' length, or "forget" to pinch a barb to ensure a big one doesn't escape. More aware than ever of the sensual and emotional gestalt of being on a river, I have moments of pure gratitude that I can still fish at all. I definitely want to be on a river often, but now I am less driven and more attuned to the risks, not just to me but to others who care about me, especially Laura, my family and closest buddies.

If you are a take-junkie like me, you know we can be crazy. In the pursuit of big fish, we can underestimate the risks and harm we could do to ourselves and loved ones. I don't want any fly fisher to go through the horrible experience I did, or put their mate, family, or buddies through it. Having experienced the fragile outer edge of my life, I can't help but give a few pieces of advice. Be very aware of the high price that can be paid for under-calculating the risk to catch that big fish. One slip, one fall, one rock to the head can ruin your fishing for a year…or an entire life. Move a little slower, more methodically, and focus on what's underfoot. Speed can kill you. Stay in shape. Keep your legs strong and regularly work on your balance. Both are critical for one's longevity in this sport. Always fish with a walkie-talkie or phone, and definitely a buddy. She or he could be your last and possibly only salvation—your "Jake."

My fourth spent life has inspired me to say "I love you" more often to my real and chosen family of friends. It has made me even more committed to my professional passion of protecting the earth. I also feel more committed to exploring new rivers and spending summers living closer to them. It has made me see our retirement savings more as a vehicle for embracing the present, including the beauty of nature, art, different cultures, good food and wine. This brush with death has made me want to write more, play more, and learn more as I age. It has truly made my mantra, "Live Now!"

Being near death has also reminded me of the randomness of fatal events, and that I could die at any time. I am now wiser and deeply aware that at one point or another, we all fall. Being fully cognizant of my mortality has made me more conscious and fully alive.

Where, when and how does the river of my life end? I don't know, but I plan to live the rest of it as if it could end in a flash, because it very well could.

Moose antlers and skull spotted in front of the Royal Coachman Lodge, Alaska, 2015, a bucket list trip

An Old Fisher's Reverie

I have had a vivid daydream that I'm going to visit an old man I have known for a long time. A few inches over five feet tall, frail, nearly bald with wild gray eyebrows, he must be in his nineties. I'm in an elder home, and before I greet him, I stop at the door and watch him in his ragged old recliner. Entranced by a book, his eyes move intensely back and forth across the pages as if looking for something. He doesn't see me, and even if he did, he wouldn't recognize me. His mind has lost its footing and only occasionally gains a solid hold long enough to remember who he is, let alone me.

On the walls around him hang framed pictures that have long ago faded from exposure to sunlight. All of his fishing buddies still surround him, at least pictorially. One stands in a stream, sleeves rolled up and rod bent as he struggles to control his wily catch. Another glances away contemplatively as he instinctively ties on a fly. Still another intently watches his fly on the river's surface. In one picture he is in his forties, kneeling, holding a huge trout with both hands and beaming an infectiously proud smile.

I say hello. He looks up from his book, and gives me a slightly curious look that asks, "Who are you and why have you come to see me?" I can tell he wants to return to his book and after a few moments he does. I wonder how it feels to know that you're alive, but not know who you are or who you were. And in moments of clarity, I ponder what it feels like when no one from your past is with you to confirm your sanity and welcome you back.

I look around the room and see no evidence that he ever reads any of the other books on the bookshelf besides the book in his hands. Tattered, discolored, and bowed, this book has obviously been read over and over and over again. A staff person walks up behind me, leans over and whispers, "He reads that same book every day." As the old man turns the final pages, I decide to wait patiently this time to let him finish; best not to interrupt him so close to the end.

His face seems to change with anticipation of something. Like a veil being pulled back, I can tell the final piece in his puzzle has fallen into place. He smiles, nods his head, and tears of joy well up. He bites his lower lip and looks up from the book, closes it, and lays it on his lap. "I know who I am," he says as he sees me for the first time. "I wrote this book." He looks at the pictures on the wall, smiles widely and tells me, "These are my friends. I wrote these stories about my life so one day I would remember who I am."

The lights in his mind turn on. He laughs and seems twenty years younger. As if he knows this moment will pass, he stands up, and with a slight bend in his stance walks around the room carefully surveying his life's mementos. He shakes his head at some pictures, at others he laughs. At one he snorts playfully, "I remember! You didn't land that fish. He broke you off!" At another he shakes his head, "I remember those moose antlers! Alaska! The best bucket list trip ever." He touches another, lowers his voice and says, "Hey, brother, how you doin' up there?" Then he opens a pretty box on the shelf and pulls out a picture of a handsome couple on their wedding day. "Such a beauty," he croons while slowly shaking his head. "I am so blessed to have loved you."

He turns away from his memories and looks straight into my eyes. He seems to recognize me. We both give each other a big warm hug and he starts to cry. "I had a good life," he whispers, his voice choking with emotion. "I had good friends. I loved my wife. I think I made a difference." I continue to hold him and let him cry. After a few minutes the tears subside, and he slips quietly into a peaceful clearing. I whisper in his ear, "It's time to go." He nods slowly and holds me tighter, as if he knows I'm referring to him. He slips from our embrace and begins to slowly make his way back to his chair. I pick up his book from the seat and help him into position. Once he's comfortable, I hand him his book, and see its title: *Life as a River*.

~~The End~~

Acknowledgments

In addition to the entire cast of characters in this book, many others contributed to it directly and indirectly, and I owe them a debt of gratitude. My Grandpa Marx was the first fisher I ever knew. My dad, Joe Marx, took me on my first fishing trip to Sheep Creek in Northeastern Washington State. My mom, Vivian, bought me my first decent rod, a Fenwick fiberglass spin caster. John Justesen created a network of well-stocked private lakes on his 19,000-acre ranch in Grass Valley, Oregon, where I learned the subtleties of lake fishing and caught the biggest trout of my life on his private stretch of a Deschutes tributary. Fishing guide, Troy Bachman, got me hooked on steelhead fishing and taught me the phrase "take junkie."

My long-time river rafting buddies, Dan Neal, Zack Lorts, Jeff Johnson, Paul Carlson, and Craig Dorsay made our many white water rafting trips on the Rogue River unforgettable. Scott Pope showed me that you can knock off fishing early and sketch a hillside or write a poem as ways to fully experience the present moment. Todd Paglia, who took the helm of ForestEthics (which later became Stand.earth) after me, and who I turned on to fly fishing, drew me to Ketchum, Idaho, to discover Ernest Hemingway's favorite river haunts. Harry Lonsdale, a second father to me and a fly fisher, convinced me to live life now. He's no longer with us, but I'm honored to be on the board of his foundation that protects the forests and rivers that he loved. Therapist Marcia Black, Ph.D., guided me through my 30's, a significant time of self-discovery and personal growth. My sisters Marie Marx Strohm and Jeannine Marx Fruci, and my brother Martin Marx deserve mention for being the greatest siblings ever and among my biggest fans, as I am theirs.

Lastly, to my editor and wife, Laura Carroll, proofreader Amanda Brown, cover designer Rob Williams, and Lisa DeSpain, who did cover design and formatting for soft cover and eBook versions of the book: My deepest thanks for helping me make this book a reality.

Answers to "Name That Fly"

Chapter	Fly
Making Rivers	Muddler Minnow, no named designer
The Kid Goes Winter Fishing	Egg TMC 105, no named designer
Awakening to the Fly	Griffiths Gnat, designed by George Griffith
It's Not Always about Catching	Dolly Llama, no named designer
Never Take a River for Granted	Creek Crawler, designed by Duane Hada
Fishing the Deschutes Stonefly Hatch	Improved Golden Stone, no named designer
Up the Rajang	Tim's Boatman, designed by Tim Drummond
The Roaring Fork River as Ally	Flashback Pheasant Tail, no named designer
Snake Medicine	Get Down Worm, designed by Bryan Robins
"Mike Marx Is Dead"	Drowned Hopper, designed by Rick Takahashi
The Odyssey: Utah, Wyoming and Idaho in a Week	Rusty Spinner, no named designer
Raised by Whales	Major Herring, designed by Thomas Kintz

The River That Cannot Be Named	Green Drake Standard, designed by Mike Lawson
My Shamanic Journey	Articulated Leech, no named designer
Fighting a Freight Train	Flashtail Mini Egg, no named designer
The Fly Fisher's Dilemma	Booms Fishing N1 Fly Fishing Trout Net - Rubber with Wood Landing Mesh Basket
Mitch: The Tao of Rivers	Skunk Green Butt, designed by Dan Callaghan
The Marriage River	Two grasshoppers, photo by BW Folsom
Tell Me a Fishing Story	Comparadun, no named designer
Fishing for Lunkers	Egg Sucking Crystal Leech, no named designer
Apocalypse Now: A River into the Heart of Darkness	Arial Assault, designed by Norm Maktima
Fishing New Zealand	Carl's Cicada, designed by Carl Stout
Unforgettable Moments in my Mental Creel	Emergent Sparkle Pupa, designed by Gay LaFontaine
Alaska: Bucket List	Mouserat, designed by Dave Whitlock
Little Boy Fishing in the Greater Yellowstone	Schroeder's Parachute Ant, designed by Ed Schroeder
When the River Ends	Hemmingway Caddis, designed by Mike Lawson
An Old Fisher's Reverie	Crystal Wing Spinner, designed by Doc Oliverio

What Does that Fly Fishing Term Mean? A Fly Fishing Glossary

Thank you to Fly Fishers International who gave permission to print many of the definitions in this glossary. Fly Fishers International's full glossary can be found at flyfishersinternational.org.

Angler: One who seeks to catch fish with a hook (an "angle"), usually fixed to the end of a line.

Back cast: The casting of line in a direction opposite to the direction the fly is intended to go. The backward counterpart of the forward cast which acts to create a bending action on the fly rod, setting up the conditions to generate the forward cast and present the fly.

Backing: The first segment of line on a reel, usually braided and used to build up the arbor and to offer additional distance for a strong fish to pull out line. An unusually strong fish will take you "into your backing."

Barb: A small triangular shaped metal at the sharp end of the hook that points in the opposite direction of the sharp end. When the fish is hooked, the barb makes it difficult for the fish to shake out the hook.*

Barbless: Barbless hooks are either manufactured without a barb or the barb is squeezed down. This feature makes it easier to remove a hook and minimizes the handling and potential damage of a fish you may want to release.

Caddis: A common aquatic insect found in many streams and rivers. They are a favorite food of trout and other fish. They have a number of distinct stages, including an underwater pupa and an above the water surface adult. Caddis have tent shaped wings and are known in both lakes and rivers to fly down upon the water to deposit their eggs.

Catch and release: A practice originating in the late 1930s to conserve fish populations by unhooking and returning a caught fish to the water in which it was caught. This is a highly successful practice in many warm water, cold water and saltwater settings.

Char: A species of fish that is related to trout that prefers cold water and is found many places in the world, including both east and west United States. Examples of Char are Brook trout, Lake trout, Arctic Char and Dolly Varden.

Dead drift: A term applied to the way that artificial flies must drift with the current to appear natural. This requires that the fly line, leader and tippet move with the fly so they don't cause unnatural drag or a "v" that will result in most fish refusing the fly.

Double haul: The term for the cast where the caster quickly pulls and releases the line on both the back cast and the forward cast.

What Does that Fly Fishing Term Mean?

It is used to create greater line speed, enabling the caster to reach farther or cut through wind.

Drag: This term has two meanings in fly fishing: (1) An unnatural pulling of a floating or submerged fly such that it moves at a different rate than the current, often (at least on the surface) creating a "V" in the water. Fish are commonly put off by drag. (2) A mechanical system that is part of a fly reel to resist and slow the speed at which line is pulled off the reel by a hooked fish.

Dropper: A practice of fishing two flies at the same time, often one on the surface and a second underwater. This increases the chances of getting a successful fly in front of a fish.

Dry fly: A fly constructed of water resistant, lightweight and buoyant materials so as to imitate an insect that alights or floats on the surface of the water.

Dun: This word has two related uses in fly fishing: (1) A grayish or grayish blue (dull) color often seen in the wings of mayfly adults, (2) An aquatic insect in a life stage just as it has emerged from the water and can fly.

Emerger: A term for an aquatic insect at the stage when it swims to the surface or just below the surface to hatch or change from a nymph or pupa to a winged adult.

False cast: Casting the fly line forward and back in the air as a means to lengthen the amount of line that extends out from the rod, to dry the fly or to modify the path of the line. In a false cast, the fly is not allowed to drop onto the water.

Feeding lane: River currents force flies into lanes on the surface or subsurface of the river. That's where the fish will often position themselves to eat in order to expend the least amount of energy. *

Float tube: Originally using a tractor or truck inner tube, this is a one-person craft with a seat across the bottom on which the fly fisher sits. Feet are in the water and scuba fins are used to move the tube around. This type of fishing boat is very popular with warm water fly fishers and with individuals who fish high mountain lakes.

Fly: An imitation of a fish food item, traditionally very light and made of hair, feathers and thread tied to a hook. Modern flies have many synthetic materials and often include lead to help them sink.

Fly fishing: A technique for fishing where the weight of the line is used to cast a very light weight fly that would not be heavy enough to be cast with a conventional spinning or casting rod.

Fly line: A line for fly fishing, originally of silk but currently made of a plastic coating over a braided line core. Fly lines are commonly 1.5 to 2 mm in diameter. The plastic coating gives the line weight and is commonly distributed unevenly to make the line easier to cast. A weight forward line, for example, has a greater plastic thickness near the forward (or fly) end of the line. Fly lines are not particularly long, generally not exceeding 105 feet. Fly lines are rated in different weights, from 1 to 11, referring to the weight of the first 30 feet of the fly line.

Fly reel: A special fishing reel with fairly simple mechanics (compared to spinning or bait casting reels) designed to hold large diameter fly line. A fly reel is relatively light and attaches below the handle on a fly rod. More sophisticated (and expensive) fly reels have a drag system that creates resistance to the rapid pulling off of line by a fish.

Fly rod: The special fishing rod constructed so as to cast a fly line. Fly rods are generally longer and thinner than spinning or casting rods. The special design involves careful attention to the way the fly rod bends because that bending action determines how well it can help cast a fly line. Fly rods were originally split cane bamboo. In the last 60 years, other materials, especially fiberglass and fiberglass with embedded graphite fibers are used. Fly rods are rated in their stiffness to match fly lines of different weights (a number 6 fly rod should be used with a number 6 fly line). See fly lines.

Freestone river: A creek or river that gets most of its water flow from rainfall or snow/glacier melt. Freestone streams are most common in mountainous regions. The name freestone refers to the fact that typical freestone streams have a bottom of stones or gravel.

Hatch: Generally refers to a stage of aquatic insect change when there is a transformation from a swimming to a fly stage and from an underwater to a surface stage. Insects in the early part of this transition are also referred to as emergers.

Hook size: To a degree hooks are standardized based upon the gap (or gape) which is defined as the distance between the hook shank and the hook point. Smaller numbers refer to larger hooks, consistent with the origin of hooks made from steel wire stock. Hooks for fly fishing range from a very small #24 (gap of 2 mm) to very large #2 (hook gap of 10 mm).

Indicator: When fishing a nymph underwater it's hard to tell when fish are taking your fly because they don't always move very far after the take. Many fly fishers attach a bit of foam, tiny rubber bobber, or even a larger dry fly far enough above the nymph to float on the surface. When the indicator pauses even slightly it may be a signal that a fish has taken the fly and it's time to set the hook.*

Leader: A single piece of tapered monofilament or multiple segments of monofilament stepped down from large where it is attached to the fly line to small where it is attached to the tippet. The butt end is usually fairly large and stiff (say 0.023 inches diameter) with the tippet end around 3X or 4X (.008-.007 inches). The section near the fly may include a tippet.

Lie: Areas in a river or lake where fish hang out, commonly well-located because they are out of the main current, present cover from predators or provide a good source of insects and other food.

Line weight: The weight of the first 30 feet of a fly line, used as a way to standardize fly lines in matching them to fly rods of differing stiffness. Line weighting is not a linear numbering system; the first 30 feet of a #6 weight line is 160 grains while the first 30 feet of a #3 weight line is 100 grains.

Mayfly: An aquatic insect found throughout the world, in both still water and rivers. It is most easily identified by its sail-like upright wings and long graceful tails. Many classic trout flies imitate mayflies. Mayflies vary in size from the 3 mm tricos to the 30 mm hexagenia.

Mend: Throwing an upstream curve into your fly line as it floats down the stream to avoid having water currents pull on it and cause unnatural movement of your fly (unnatural drift or line drag). Fish and especially trout are exquisitely sensitive to (and turned off by) movement of an insect that moves at a different rate or in a different direction than the current.

Midge: A very small (non-biting), two-winged insect, related to deer flies, mosquitos and craneflies.

Nymph: An underwater stage of aquatic insect. It is an important source for all varieties of warm water and cold water fish.

Pool: A reach or segment of a river or stream with greater depth and slower current, making it safer from predator birds and animals and where swimming against the current is reduced.

Pupa: An intermediate stage of certain insects, generally the stage between the larva and adult form of caddis flies or midges. Also refers to the fly imitation of these insects.

Redd: The hollowed out nest in a streambed where a fish deposits its eggs, a behavior typical to most salmonids.

Riffle: A part of the river where it is shallower and the rocks on the bottom create more surface turbulence and faster water. Riffles are often more oxygenated due to the turbulence and support many bugs because of the oxygen and the rocks to which they can attach themselves. Both of these factors make riffles excellent for holding trout.*

Rise: The action of a fish as it comes to the surface of the water to feed. Different kinds of rises (splashy, dimpled, etc.) suggest different kinds of feeding and may suggest different kinds of insects.

Run: This term has two meanings in fly fishing: (1) A section of stream where relatively shallow water goes over a rough or gravel bottom and then into a pool. (2) The pulling out of line a hooked fish makes in trying to escape.

Setting the hook: To make sure the hook penetrates the fish's mouth, an angler must apply an upward motion of the fly rod or some sort of quick tension on the fly line. When fishing with artificial lures and flies, fish often do not hook themselves because very soon after they "mouth" the fly, they are aware that it does not feel, taste or smell like it should. They will spit it out. This puts a premium on setting the hook at the right time.

Skein: A cluster of fish eggs held together inside a thin translucent membrane.*

Spawn: The behavior of fish where females deposit eggs (also called spawn) on various surfaces (varying with species) and the male produces necessary milt (fish sperm) to ultimately turn the eggs into fry (young fish).

Spin casting rod: This is a rod that uses only monofilament nylon line, not a fly line. It is generally used to cast lures or spinners (metal imitations of minnows or small fish) or bait (worms, grasshoppers, small bait fish) and has a reel which can be set to easily release line as the rod is quickly whipped forward, propelling the lures/bait and line.*

Spring creek: A creek or stream that gets its water from a ground flow or spring sources, rather than glacier/snow melt or surface run off. Spring creeks are generally at a temperature of the average rainfall temperature over the course of the year (the source of most ground water) and hence usually do not warm significantly in the summer nor freeze in the winter.

Stonefly: An aquatic insect found throughout North America that generally requires higher water quality than most fish, including trout. It varies in size, but in the larger sub-species can reach 2 inches. Its life stages vary from mayflies and caddis flies inasmuch as it crawls out of the water onto a rock, splits its outer covering and becomes a flying insect with wings that lay on its back.

Streamer: A fly classically made of long soft feathers or animal hair (like bucktail) to imitate a bait fish, leech or other non-insect. Modern streamers are made of many synthetic materials, including metallic film and even epoxy.

Strike: The action of a fish in trying to eat a fly. This term also refers to the movement of the rod a fly angler makes to set the hook.

Stripping: Bringing in a fly line with a series of short or varied pulls so as to simulate a living insect or bait fish or to maintain tension on a hooked fish. Stripping often also involves movements of the rod tip.

Tailwater: The downstream section of a river or stream found below a large man-made dam. The most famous and productive tailwaters are from bottom-discharge dams, making the water relatively cold and constant in temperature.

Terrestrial insect: As the name implies, these are land-dwelling (or tree/plant-dwelling) insects that breathe air, including grasshoppers, crickets, ants, beetles and leaf worms.

Tippet: The terminal segment of monofilament tied on the end of a leader and connected to the fly.

Waders: Footed trousers that are constructed of latex, neoprene, Gortex or other waterproof material so as to keep anglers dry. Currently waders come in stocking foot or booted form and can be found in three lengths: hip waders, waist-high waders and chest waders.

Wading staff: A walking stick especially adapted to provide stability to a wading fly angler when moving through fast or deep water. Some wading staffs are foldable and can be kept in a fishing vest pocket until needed.

Wild native trout: Wild means they were born in the river, not in a hatchery. Not all wild trout are native. Native means the trout are indigenous to that river or lake and have been there possibly for centuries or millennia. They may be the progeny of non-native fish planted years earlier that were able to spawn and reproduce naturally. Wild native trout are the crème de la crème for fly fishing purists.*

X diameter: A system to indicate the diameter of leader and tippet material, with 0X (zero-X) representing the largest diameter (.011 inches) and 8X (.003 inches) representing a small, light diameter. Commonly used values are 1X (.010), 2X (.009), 3X (.008), 4X (.007), 5X (.006), 6X (.005). The strength of these monofilament diameters varies with the kind of material.

*This is a fly fishing term used in this book and defined by Michael Marx.

www.ingramcontent.com/pod-product-compliance
Lightning Source LLC
Chambersburg PA
CBHW052016290426
44112CB00014B/2265